BE
HOLD
ING

FOREWORD BY JOHN MARK COMER

DEEPENING OUR
EXPERIENCE IN GOD

BE
HOLD
ING

STRAHAN
COLEMAN

DAVID C COOK

transforming lives together

BEHOLDING
Published by David C Cook
4050 Lee Vance Drive
Colorado Springs, CO 80918 U.S.A.

Integrity Music Limited, a Division of David C Cook
Brighton, East Sussex BN1 2RE, England

The graphic circle C logo is a registered trademark of David C Cook.

The website addresses recommended throughout this book are offered as a
resource to you. These websites are not intended in any way to be or imply an
endorsement on the part of David C Cook, nor do we vouch for their content.

Bible credits are listed in the back of the book.

Library of Congress Control Number 2022943197
ISBN 978-0-8307-8518-6
eISBN 978-0-8307-8519-3

© 2023 Strahan Coleman
Published in association with The Bindery Agency, www.TheBinderyAgency.com.

The Team: Michael Covington, Stephanie Bennett,
Elise Boutell, Jack Campbell, Susan Murdock
Cover Design: James Hershberger

Printed in the United States of America
First Edition 2023

1 2 3 4 5 6 7 8 9 10

101222

For Jude, already held.

CONTENTS

FOREWORD

Deep in the subterranean recesses of every human heart is an *ache*—for God, for Love, for Beauty, for a Peace to stand against the sea of chaos. Pascal called it the "God-shaped hole." The inner void we *all* seek to fill.

Not long ago, in the heyday of secularism's seeming triumph over Christianity in the West, this idea of a God-shaped hole seemed like a quaint myth, believed upon by preachers of the gospel, scoffed at by (equally ardent) preachers of Western-style secularism. Look at the "lost," they claimed. They aren't moping around in existential angst whilst reading Nietzsche on Sunday morning instead of repenting of sin at church; they are out to brunch with friends, reveling in the lifestyle of the upwardly mobile, free to eat and drink and believe and say and do and sleep with whoever or whatever they want—is there a greater happiness?

Now *that* feels like the quaint myth. As Jesus once put it, "Wisdom is justified by her children." The mirage of a God-free happy life has burned off in the fire of the last decade. In its place we have the rise and fall of Donald Trump, the worldwide chaos and loss of 2020, a global uprising over systemic racism, an opioid crisis, a mental health epidemic, spiking rates of all the harbingers of doom—crime, murder, suicide, sexual assault, addiction, etc. And in the ashes of Covid's worldwide purge, where have people turned? To identity politics. To conspiracy theories. To militant secularisms on the Left and the Right. To religions, no less than Christianity, but religions without Love. Dogmas that divide into us vs. them, that stoke anger and ire, that decimate peace and disseminate fear, that promise the heaven of _____ and leave millions in the wake of disillusionment and despair.

But behind all the rage, the ache is still there, gnawing at the human heart. Across continents and creeds.

My friend Strahan has written a liturgy for the ache; he's put lyrics and music and melody to the deepest desire of the heart—the desire for God. Not just to know *about* God, as the cliché goes, but to *know* God, by direct experience. To experience emotionally what is true of us theologically by the cross and the coming of the Spirit: that we are "in Christ." (Which is the best definition of contemplation I know.) Strahan is a fellow contemplative; we share the same ache. We met years ago on a trip to New Zealand, and he was immediately a kindred spirit, a soul on a similar journey to God. This book tells his story and, in a way, writes a new story for the rest of us.

Many generations ago, the prophet Jeremiah said, "Stand at the crossroads and look; ask for the ancient paths, ask where the good way is, and walk in it, and you will find rest for your souls."[1] Strahan is one who has found the ancient paths. Like all the great saints and sages down through church history, he discovered it not in a library or university classroom, but on a bed of suffering, in his case, literally. He "let perseverance finish its work," and it enriched his soul with wisdom and insight into the path to God.[2] As he rested, he found rest.

The path to "rest for your souls" is, as it's always been, the path of true prayer. A prayer that goes beyond asking God for what we want, to letting God become what we most desire—a prayer of letting go as much as reaching out to grasp. Upon this path, our Shepherd is Jesus Himself, our road is healing from the wounding of sin, and our destination is union with the God who is Love.

So, read this book, yes, but I think Strahan himself would say: that's not the point. The book is an on-ramp; the call is to the path, to the Way, to the journey with—and to—the Father, the Son, and the Holy Spirit. This book is just the next step ...

John Mark Comer
Bridgetown Church / Practicing The Way

Introduction

AN INVITATION

Saturdays were never quiet days in the Coleman household. Not only because my older brother and I weren't prone to sitting around passively, but if my dad was home, there was music playing.

My dad loves music. He grew up collecting records spanning Black Sabbath to James Taylor, and in the '90s he filled our bookshelf with CDs. Dad would ramp up the volume whilst working around the property doing whatever he needed to do, and if you peeked around the corner, you'd often see him pumping the air with an invisible guitar. It felt like every album he put on was his favourite. But more than just listening, he always felt the music. It was bone-deep for him.

It was contagious too. I was only eight when I started writing songs myself, and on weekends, I too would sit around letting the music sink deep down into me. Now, looking back, I credit Dad's energy for music with inspiring my own. I caught the feeling of what it could do, I felt it, and I ended up spending the first half of my professional life sharing it with others through my own songs around the world.

Our greatest passions are often caught, not taught. That's what this book is about. Not loud music and artistic career, but about catching the heart of an adventure into the unending magnitude and love of God. And then living our entire lives that way.

Despite what it may feel like at times, I believe there really is a deep longing for genuine and permanent renewal in our generation. To catch a vision for the Christ-life that sets us on a lifelong holy trajectory. For many, as the world has become a more complex place, the longing for a simple, yet transformative, Christian experience has grown with it. Amidst a globalised and hyper-connected world where facts appear to have eroded into subjectivity, a renewed deep cry for meaning and truth has grown. That longing may at times lead people *from* the church rather than *toward* her, but the desire remains.

The world longs for God.

No one is without this divine ache—whether they realise it or not. Humanity was built to be dependent on the operating system of Divine Communion, and when the world becomes louder and more vitriolic, the ache for that communion only increases. God isn't merely a good idea or a meal ticket to an eternal banquet, He is the very essence and origin of pleasure, goodness, excitement, adventure, joy, and wonder. Not just because we find those things in what He gives us, but because we find those things in God Himself. He is absolute perfect and unimaginably satisfying goodness. Being with Him is rest, hydration, and freedom.

Prayer is a word we use to broadly name that experience and the many ways we seek to satisfy this holy longing. It's for each generation to explore what meeting that ache looks like. It's part of the torch handed down to us for centuries from the earliest church.

We were created to feel God in our bones like this. To live in the wide-eyed wonder of a life caught up and surrounded by Him, and yet often it can feel like life with God, and prayer, is hard, dry work. If prayer is the road on which we travel to God, then a crisis of prayer is also a crisis for our God-ache. If the longing is for the soul's deep thirst to be satisfied, then theology, cultural analysis, or revived church community is not enough. We need God Himself. We need to rediscover how to know Him.

We can genuinely believe that God is good and worthy of all our attention, we can say with our minds that He is always with us and never ceases to love, and yet the reality of it can sometimes feel as though it's a multiverse away. A reality that others feel, not us. For us, prayer may feel tiring and like it's more of a chore than a pleasure, more anxiety inducing than restful. And just as painfully, all the theological head stuff often doesn't make much of a dent on our being loving, kind, generous, gentle, and joyful. Knowledge alone can't change us.

We can go to church for decades, serve in missions teams, pastor and preach even, and yet find ourselves at the end of it all depleted, unsure, not feeling as if we know the God we offer others.

The music of our faith becoming all scales and rehearsals. No dancing dad.

French aviator and writer Antoine de Saint-Exupéry is credited for saying, "If you want to build a ship, don't drum up people to collect wood and don't assign them tasks and work, but rather teach them to long for the endless immensity of the sea."[3] This book is my attempt at showing you something of that endless sea. It's about prayer becoming a place of adventure and wonder, something you can't live without because it's so deeply satisfying. Because God is.

It's about us becoming *beholders*.

Beholding is prayer, but it's much more than that too. It's about holy existence. It takes prayer out of the small pockets of conscious mental dialogue and makes it a life lived out fully in the Trinity.

Beholding is the practice of gazing into God, gazing into us, gazing back into Him. Our Christian ancestors used the language of placing our minds in our hearts and learning to pray from there. David expressed this as his soul's singular ambition in Psalm 27:4:

> One thing I ask from the LORD,
>   this only do I seek:
> that I may dwell in the house of the LORD
>   all the days of my life,
> to gaze on the beauty of the LORD
>   and to seek him in his temple.

Beholding is a life founded on the truth that no other offer on earth or in heaven is greater than that of simply staring into the eternal eyes of God, then seeing our world through them. It places a great value on God Himself; it makes Him that worth our time. Yet as I hope to show you, practising beholding transforms our relationships, the way we see our bodies, the church, others, and the world too.

The language of prayer can sometimes conjure ideas of work, striving, and fixed agendas. It can seem as if we're being asked to do more to see change. But that's the very notion of life and prayer that I hope to challenge. I want to re-beautify the idea of prayer as communion with God, and give testimony to the foundation of love as it was always meant to be so that we come to mean something different, or at least much deeper, when we say *prayer*.

Prayer is the birthplace of our deepest knowing and creativity. It offers us the profound simplicity we need—a simplicity that can flow beneath all the complexity of our world and our sense-making of it; a simplicity that sustains us. Because our relationship to God shapes our relationship with all others and the world around us. Get that right, and our lives tend to follow. How we pray affects everything—our study, our theology, our view of those who aren't like us, our view of ourselves, our use of material resources, our treatment of the created environment—and ultimately shapes who we are becoming.

But I'm not sure we've been teaching prayer that way on the whole. Often prayer is taught only in the context of praying *for* things. It's the place we seek forgiveness, provision, or world peace, not holy recreation. I can't help but feel our inability to see prayer as a place of abiding rather than achievement has driven a performance culture in the church and robbed many of us from the spiritual fruits Christ promised us.

By reforming the culture of our prayer, by opening a space wide enough to embrace being *with* God as much as being *for* Him, by returning our hearts to our first love, reshaping the language and practice of how we approach God, and rediscovering the art of beholding, I believe we'll find fresh water and sustenance for the times we live in. We'll draw water from the deep wells that have kept God's faithful nourished for millennia past.

And that brings us here, to today. Sometimes when we read a book like this, we assume the author has perfected the subject in their life. That's far from the truth with me. I'm sharing what I've seen, not what I've perfected. I penned much of this in the turbulent years of 2020–21 and felt like I was relearning a lot of it in the process. I know that journey will never end for me.

My hope is that we can help each other encounter a way of being and seeing that grounds our faith in ways we've only dreamed. I know I'll be spending the rest of my life putting into practice the reality of what I'm sharing with you; I'm no professional pray-er and don't plan to be. I'm not sure we're ever meant to be.

In a way, this is me sharing my return to the wonder-eyed youth that stared into the stars and saw God. This time, though, I'm gazing from the other side of some of the trials and challenges life delivers. From those early years until now, I've dedicated my life to prayer and the pursuit of God and still feel like I'm only an inch deep in the bottomless adventure of Him.

That's why I'm sharing this with you. Because if the small revelation that came through my own struggles and suffering to fall into God can help you sink a few millimeters deeper in your own search for Him, or if it opens your eyes even a little more to God's irrevocable withness in your life, then it's a valuable endeavour.

I hope you'll see this book as an invitation from God to stop and stew for a while in the hope of deeper divine communion. Like how my seeing Dad being engrossed in music helped change the course of my life, I hope that in these pages you might catch a glimpse of God that would do the same for you.

I've dedicated my life to prayer and the pursuit of God and still feel like I'm only an inch deep in the bottomless adventure of Him.

If you will, allow me to be just another pilgrim beside you on the road to divine intimacy, sharing the things I've seen along my own path in the hope it may encourage you on yours.

Like Elijah in the wilderness, when the thunder, wind, and fires of the world and of our lives rage, we're invited to retreat into the still, small whisper; a whisper that draws us into quiet simplicity rather than competing ambition, and leads us to the discovery of a patient God, who in His gentleness can and will transform a generation.

The invitation here is to simple friendship. It is to prayer as a satisfying and abiding pleasure. It's to the remapping of our expectations about where our strength comes from, a call to exhale into the unburdening God and to inhale His beauty and life.

In the midst of our present global confusion, there is a Presence engulfing enough to sweep up the inner pain we face and give hope in times of despair. There is a Comfort for the disoriented and those who search for meaning, and there is a Way that leads to life in all its fullness.

It's not a new way; it's an ancient one. It's the way of love, adoration, and devotion. It is the way, the art, of beholding. And only God can lead us there.

Come, Holy Spirit,
And show us our Father,
Our life source, our longing,
Our home.

Chapter 1

DISCOVERING BEHOLDING

"Jesus, faithful, Holy-Carpenter,
You bring meaning out of broken things—
severed things—those lonely branches
amidst the untamed forest."

Prayer Vol. 01

"I begged You for employment;
You offered me friendship.
I assumed Your distance;
You presumed our intimacy."

Prayer Vol. 02

"I no longer call you servants ... now I call you friends."[4]

Jesus Christ

I've searched for God my whole life. As I look back, wonder of Him was effortless when I was a child. I would look up at the stars and somehow know, even deeply feel, that He was simultaneously up there in the vastness and down here in my minuteness. Created things told me that. The world was too expansive and beautiful to have come about without love and intention. God hid among it, waiting to be discovered.

As I grew into my teens, if you'd asked me in a word to describe God, I would have said "beautiful" without even considering whether there were more important words. I have no idea where that came from. Reflecting on it now, it's obvious God put it there. Children intuit things we fight so much harder for as adults.

My later teen years were marked with a hunger to be able to harness that sense, and to truly know God. Prayer was like a steam engine driving me toward Him, sometimes out of desire, other times out of frustration and confusion. But the longer you live, the longer you think, which for me at least meant overthinking. What was easy as a child, looking up to the stars and feeling God, felt mistier as I grew older. I began to see the world in varying shades, and found myself asking more questions of God than I was getting answers to.

Prayer turned to fasting, late night prayer meetings, and Pentecostal fervour as I broached my twenties. I was hungry, starving even, to reach the point where occasional prayer turned into continual union. I was reaching upward with everything I had, becoming increasingly frustrated that my efforts couldn't quite deliver. Prayer slowly felt like speaking into nothingness and less like wonder.

Around that same time in my twenties, I was beginning a painful mental descent. This Beauty I was chasing, though it consumed my desire, seemed more and more untouchable. I had unexplainable bouts of heaviness that threw me for sometimes months at a time. A friend going through a bad break-up once shared that the loneliness made him feel like a "cosmic orphan." I loved that; it spoke exactly to how I felt at times with God.

God would punctuate my life with moments of His love and presence, but I didn't know how to build a life container deep within me for the kind of relationship with Him that I knew I was made for. It wasn't enough to see visions, have dreams, or experience powerful sung worship moments only to wake up the next morning feeling unsure how to find that very same God in my ordinary life. That ache for a union with Beauty beyond ministry and the "doing" stuff moved from a dull ache to a desperate hope.

Then in 2015, my body started shutting down on me. I'd been touring as a musicianary for several years with my wife, Katie, taking leaps of faith across continents and following the Spirit's invitation to love those who didn't yet know Him. We were giving it everything when my body decided that it had had enough of healthy operating and slowly gave way to frequent sickness and, in turn, a depth of depression and anxiety that I had never reached before.

For a number of years, I spent the majority of my time in bed or too unwell to work for one reason or another. I got every virus you could think of, often back to back for six months during winter. My head constantly spun, and I lived with an enduring mental fog. I was spending hundreds of dollars a week on vitamins that my body refused to absorb.

During that time, I forced myself up and spent days at a Franciscan retreat centre on the east coast of Auckland. I couldn't do much, but I would journal, look out the window, sleep on single beds in the guest rooms, and just be silent and still before God. Back then, it was enough for me just to exist, and to exist in front of God. It was all I could really do.

But it wasn't all quiet and nice. There were plenty of days when I would crawl on the floor and rage at God, asking how He could allow this to happen when I had devoted my life to Him. I begged Him for an answer. The Psalms and their prayerful wrestling became a treasure to me like never before. All the while, I lost my wonder, and that union with God I longed for felt more and more distant. It was hard to love a God who stood by as my life fell apart. Especially after everything I'd done for Him.

Though it didn't help one bit, I tried my best to hide the depths of both my physical struggle and my emotional struggle from those around me. I couldn't explain it to them, so I hardly tried. The doctors could never give it a name, and at times I wondered if I was just making it all up.

It wasn't just the sickness either. Before all this started, we'd lived a somewhat miraculous life. Genuinely. We'd lived literally week to week in faith trusting God would feed us and pay our bills whilst we lived out our calling. It felt like we always had a story to tell of incredible financial provision, miraculous global connections, dreams in the night that came true the next week, and stories of healing and deliverance through my songs at shows.

Then, it was like overnight, all of that just ceased. The provision ended, the stories stopped, the miraculous connections dissipated. Cars, dishwashers, computers, and hot water cylinders broke down for nothing. It was like living in a weird horror movie. A few Christians close to me actually said they thought I was cursed. This was a full-blown spiritual and mental health crisis. And it just kept going and going.

Living in that kind of confusion and chaos doesn't make prayer or closeness with God very easy. If my mind becomes the battleground, how can I open up to God in any real way? If prayer is about conscious mental dialogue with God, what do I do when dialogue of any kind is difficult, let alone with a Being who has all the answers but, it seems, is refusing to give any?

Existence was hard enough without the existential madness of sharing it with God. My theology was being shaken and shattered, and I didn't know how to commune with Someone who no longer made any sense to me. Was true communion something only those with a clear enough mind or enough physical strength could have? Suddenly I felt very "unspiritual." God was in the dark.

But then something important happened. I gave up.

I gave up on being able to pray, on understanding what was going on with me, on waiting for it all to be fixed, and on needing answers. I gave up on trying to perform my way into God's heart too. It started to dawn on me almost three years into this crisis that what I was experiencing might not just be a blip on the map of life. That this—the illnesses, the mental overwhelm, the frustration—could be part of my existence for the rest of my life, and so, what was I going to do about it? Was all this really power-ful enough to limit union with God? Was Jesus' life, death, and resurrection under threat from my feelings of cosmic orphancy and persistent brain fog? Or could I commune with God there in the midst of it, even without healing, answers, or a clear mind?

When I thought about it, though this new existence didn't line up with the charismatic expectations of life in God's kingdom I'd had as a younger man, I was noticing a different sense of God in my life. One not built around felt sense, but a growing, insistent trust that He was there somehow. There in a loving way.

I was slowly learning that God either loved me or He didn't, and if my ability to pray well, do good Christian things, or live some idealized way had more power to affect that love than my simply existing, then I couldn't do anything about it in my pres-ent, unable state. I couldn't control my situation, and God didn't seem to want to give me answers for it either, so I had to make a decision: Would I stay offended by God's seeming silence and absence amidst my horror, or would I choose to look for and know Him in the midst of my frustration and despair?

I vividly remember the morning I decided. It was during a low month, and in those times, I used to force my fatigued body out of the house and down to the cafe nearby as a ritual for keeping some semblance of normality in a life of physical lack. It was a chilled but sunny spring morning, and the ascending sun reflected light off the shop windows at sharp angles along the main road. I was sitting in the bench window seat with my espresso, tensed up as usual, thinking about what to say to God. As often was the case, my prayer could have gone one of two ways—anger or relent.

That day I chose relent, and I wrote in my prayer journal, "Thank You, God, for my life." I then prayed, "Father, if this is it, if this is what my life will look like till the day I die—financially strapped, vocationally stuffed, relationally strained, and medically confused—then it's okay. I have You, I have life, I have this beautiful world and my beautiful family. Let me be alive to enjoy and behold You whatever may come." It was a prayer of acceptance.

---

*Would I stay offended by God's seeming silence
and absence, or would I choose to look for Him
in the midst of my frustration and despair?*

Something lifted, something I'd been carrying for a long, long time. I don't even know what it was precisely, but it felt like the equivalent of a sports stadium floated off my chest with the ease of a down pillow. Maybe it was my dependence on understanding as a prerequisite to truly experiencing God. Maybe it was my realising that external things couldn't control my internal world. Or maybe it was my acknowledgement that God really was close in that season. Wherever the lift came from, it was the beginning of learning to let God be God, and to not allow my confusion to be the focus of our relationship anymore.

The immediate side effect was that my prayer life carried less mental hardship, less striving for God, for healing, for answers, for release. Instead, prayer became more just sitting in front of Him watching, learning to discover the beauty that was already present to me. It wasn't about giving up on my questions and needs, but they were no longer the be-all and end-all of my adoring God.

I still talked to Him about my suffering and was more honest than ever, but we talked about it now within the confines of beholding love. Letting God be Himself allowed me to be more truly myself also. Prayer was no longer work. It was becoming recreation.

I knew I didn't need to hold my punches any longer with God because I wasn't trying to impress Him anymore. I finally realised I didn't really have much to impress Him with anyway. And because my life was constantly shrinking as I was able to do less and less, there was little left to ask God to do aside from healing myself or others. Prayer became the whole point of my faith, and the whole point of prayer became being together. I had a lot of downtime then, and as it turns out, so does He.

A strange thing happens when we decentralize asking in our prayer life. What do we do? How do we commune with God without agenda or necessity? I wonder if the answer is partly why so many of us pray like crazy in suffering, then forget about God in healing, because we don't know what to do when the basis of our relationship is no longer desperate acceptance, healing, longing, or need.

This was my crisis, but you may have your own. It may be more or less drastic. It may just be the persistent ache of wishing God felt closer more often or the sense that prayer is exhausting, hard work or a chore. Over the years of telling my story, I've come to understand that so many of us have had to wrestle with what it means to *be* with God.

Because when the dust settles on our questions, frustration, deconstruction, suffering, or numbness, what's left is a desire to reclaim that wonder—that beauty—again. What rises to the surface is the deep longing to behold and be beheld by God.

During those years, my life with God became about watching Him, watching life, and accepting who He is even when He offended me by not healing, not changing, not providing, and not answering. God never did tell me why I went through what I did, or why He felt quiet all those years. But He did tell me He loved me, and I learned to accept that as enough.

How do we commune with God without agenda or necessity? I wonder if the answer is partly why so many of us pray like crazy in suffering, then forget about God in healing, because we don't know what to do when the basis of our relationship is no longer desperate acceptance, healing, longing, or need.

My need to know and understand what God was doing in my life in order to trust and admire Him was dethroned. I began to love God and trust His goodness aside from the chaos of my life. Aside from the good things too.

In the years since that experience sitting in the cafe window, I have had less and less to say. I sit more with God, letting Him be. I let Him be Mystery, Wonder, Grace, Goodness, and Truth, despite whether I understand it or not. This isn't an ecstatic experience, but an ordinary, humanising one. My feelings didn't necessarily change, but that mattered less because I could behold God without depending on my emotions.

On days when depression and despair consumed me, I was able to lie there and say to myself, "God is still God today, still beautiful, still wonderful, still loving," and sit in my darkness knowing that my feelings couldn't change that reality. God was among my feelings, but I was finally learning that God is more than a feeling. He's God.

Without my noticing it, I gradually changed. Weirdly, though I didn't have the mind space to ask for such things as patience, kindness, gentleness, or long-suffering, I began to embody them in new ways. I softened in my interactions with my wife, my children, my friends, and those others in the world who had felt like unlovable strangers to me in the past. As I learned to let God be Himself without making sense of my circumstances, I wept over people who I had previously considered enemies. People I couldn't understand. I was losing all my enemies. All I could see now was God.

I was changing, and my prayer life was too. As I began to feel this unity with Beauty, I simultaneously felt connected in love and friendship with every other person—like I could see God in them more clearly. Like we were all just little children, some more lost than others. Beholding God came to mean beholding the other.

Learning to sit and let God be God, learning to experience the world with this kind of tender mystery, irrevocably transformed my life. It removed the power of sickness, division, despair, and hopelessness. My world wasn't free of those things, but they became peripheral issues.

It was like I was falling in love with God again. Not with a naive first love, but an older, deeper, and more truthful love. Like we were both seeing each other for who we were for the first time, not who we wished the other was. Except, it was me, not God, who was finally waking up. Prayer became existence. Existence became beautiful. I realised I'd been praying in reverse my whole life, looking for a working relationship when God longed for a friend.

Beholding prayer saved my spiritual life.

Chapter 2

RELEARNING
TO BREATHE

*"You're not a product to be consumed,
but a wonder to behold.
Father, make me Your beholder."*

Prayer Vol. 02

*"You look me in the eyes, Father,
and give me Your full attention.
Teach me how to do the same with You,
and to live life more present to my Maker."*

Prayer Vol. 02

*"One thing have I asked of the LORD ...
that I may dwell in the house of the LORD
all the days of my life,
to gaze upon the beauty of the LORD."*[5]

King David

To overcome the brute force tidal pull of a love-depleted world, we need a reformation of vision. We need a way through all the noise and transaction-like interactions we experience every day to discover the God who sits kindly among us and the tiny details of our lives. A way to discover a deeper divine communion. This way is found, I believe, in beholding—a way of prayer that dignifies God, giving Him special space among us in the face of all this noise.

Prayer is always a loaded word, so what I'm meaning when I'm saying *prayer* is a way of being with and seeing God amidst the process of our moving through the world. Calling it *prayer* feels limiting because often when we use that word, we're thinking about techniques or continuous conscious mental dialogue. But beholding is deeper.

It's about how we hold God before us and how we live from the place of being held by Him. It's the practice of looking to God with an open soul, admiring Him, allowing Him to be, and watching Him move in and around our lives. It's a much wider definition than speaking to God to get things done, offering words of praise, or interceding on behalf of others. It's about how we exist.

In a way, it's praying without ceasing, but it's also more than that. It's about spending our lives admiring the beauty of God, without agenda. To be with God in this way, without special outcomes or objectives, is to love Him for Him alone. It's in itself a holy life. It's our response to the Great Commandment.

Because of all this, beholding prayer fundamentally restructures our relationship with God from a working partnership to a divine friendship.

Throughout the centuries, monks, priests, disciples, mystics, and pundits alike have all sought to give language to how we can look upon God in a beholding way. The greatest expression of this idea is found in the many beautiful writings of the Desert Fathers and Mothers and the history of contemplative spirituality. But that's not where the penny dropped for me. For me, learning the language of beholding God came one September morning whilst I looked out at a diamond glass ocean as the sun emerged over the horizon.

Each day during the many years when I was unwell, I would, when I could, stroll along a concrete walkway on the beach where we lived. It's amazing to me how the same place can present so differently each day depending on the light. This particular morning was symphonic.

The harmony of the breeze, the sun, the fresh smells of autumn in Aotearoa, New Zealand, and the dancing diamonds on the tips of the water's wake overwhelmed me. I stopped. I couldn't say anything. My heart soaked it up like a sponge and swelled within me. It was mystical, and I could feel God there. I was stunned to stillness. Then, an unwelcome undoing began.

Beholding prayer restructures our relationship with God from a working partnership to a divine friendship.

The second I became self-aware of what was happening, I started to panic. I tried to make more of the moment, to really "feel" it. Maybe I could write a song about it, maybe I was meeting God and He was about to speak? *These pure moments don't come often*, I thought, *I've got to make the most of it.*

Then my thoughts turned to the horrible fact that I couldn't just enjoy the beauty of this moment. I needed to greedily eke more feelings out of it, or some kind of extra spiritual value, to capitalise on it, take a photo, or think about what it all meant. I felt like an idiot juggling a hot potato, except this potato was the opportunity to behold a beautiful world.

Suddenly, in the middle of all this interior madness, the Spirit interrupted, "Son, this is exactly what you're like with Me. Always looking to make more out of our time together, to feel more, to get answers, to grow, or to understand. But aren't I as worthy of stunned-silent admiration as this view? Isn't it enough to be engulfed in My beauty and goodness and to behold Me? Isn't that in itself worthy of the moment?"

God was right, of course. How willing I had always been to admire a song, stare at a piece of masterful art, weep at the birth of my children, or just sit quietly in the haze of an orange sunset. But how rarely had I seen prayer that way. My default approach to prayer was as a place to pass important information and requests between God and me rather than seeing it as a place to simply stare in wonder at the beauty and mystery of God. To waste time on and with Him.

Painfully, I was realising that in one way or another, I had only consumed God. I had subconsciously sought Him merely for answers, blessing, peace, or emotional experience and called that worship. I'd been a taker in prayer, less a giver-admirer, and I had learned enough by then to know that's not how love is meant to be.

GOD IS NOT A PRODUCT AND NEITHER ARE YOU

Like an invisible weed, the spirit of consumerism has crept into how many of us pray, and it's not really a surprise. Over the last few centuries, as industrialisation and globalisation have taken root in the world, both Western culture and its church have had major worldview shifts.

Before the Industrial Revolution, products were connected to people. We used to be able to tell who had made the shirts we wore and built the chairs we sat in. Most things we owned had a story attached to them, a person. We felt a connection to the things that added value to our lives and we owned fewer of them.

But that changed with the mass production of the Industrial Revolution. Suddenly, the story of a thing became less important and what mattered instead was getting the best possible product at the lowest price and in the fastest time. This became the consumerism culture that you and I breathe every day. The result? What we value slowly slipped from those who provide our things to the things they provide.

The religion of consumerism sees possessions, creation, and even other people as a means to our personal gain. We hardly think twice anymore about climbing the corporate ladder (consuming our own natural gifts and vocations), making money from relationships (capitalising influencer culture and social media cult communities), or promoting our adventurous side (leveraging the attention of others for our own status) through endless photos of our holidays and personal endeavours. We've made it a habit to consume products without care for the conditions and circumstances of their makers, becoming more and more disconnected from the consequences of our material appetites.

In turn, this way of seeing the world, this disconnection between product and person, has seeped into our spirituality, radically affecting how we see and experience God.

Many of us have come to consume God as a way of achieving the best possible life, at the lowest possible cost, and at our earliest convenience. We may not say it that way, but the theology of consumerism subtly underlies much of the way we see the world, experience church, and sadly, how we pray.

For so many of us, the harsh reality is that it's not so much God we want as the security, emotional experiences, sense-making, or community He gives us. This shows up in our prayers as the product over the Producer. Consumeristic prayer is transactional only. It's about give and take: worship for blessings, or repentance for shame-lifting. The result is a view of prayer that is primarily centred on getting things done or getting what we want with tangible outcomes or personal gain, rather than sitting with and admiring God. It limits our relationship with the God of beauty to a working relationship.

Consumer prayer also limits our relationship with God to the state of our emotions, and though God is fully among our emotions, He also longs to be greater than them to us. To pray and worship *only* when we feel like it or when we want to feel something is spiritual consumerism and so is rating the quality of our time with Him based on how it made us feel. Beholding God and feeling God aren't mutually exclusive, of course, but in a culture that looks to feelings for spiritual validation, reclaiming true prayer when it doesn't benefit our emotions is as important as ever.

Over the years in marriage, I've learned that many of the greatest displays of our truest love come from times when we feel it least. Because the truth is, when we really *feel* like it, love is easy, not selfless. But living out our love when we don't feel like it, that's when we test whether we love the person or what they give us. That's when our love grows up.

What we value slowly slipped from those who provide our things to the things they provide.

Marriage (and really all forms of covenanted relationships like friendships and communities) tests that kind of love-selfish relationship. Because if you spend enough time with people, there will be days when you're either too tired, ratty, self-absorbed, or anxious to want to worry about anyone else, and yet others may still need you. If a tit-for-tat love is all we have in those moments, relationships crumble. But if we're able to push through the vacuum of feelings to serve someone else's needs before our own, the true fruit of love is found in us.

In the same way, salvation is a divine marriage and prayer is the art of showing up daily out of a love that moves deeper than feelings.

When we behold, we transcend spiritual consumerism. We're no longer primarily interested in what God could change in our lives, or the lives of others, or how He can be of service to us. Feelings and spiritual ascent aren't our priority anymore; admiring and perceiving Mystery is, and that's an entirely different longing altogether.

Because in that space, in the space of beholding prayer, we're allowed to not feel anything and still consider our time best spent. We're welcome to not understand, and in fact our worried minds are reminded of the truth that unclarity can be precisely a sign that we've touched God.

Strange as it may sound, when we talk about beholding God, we don't mean consuming Him. We mean admiring Him, and there is an important difference. A deep enjoyment of God as He is will often mean we'll experience pleasure, peace, joy, and love when we're spending time with Him. But beholding prayer values its time with God even when none of that is present, which matters in seasons when we can't trust our feelings, or when we're moving through the unwelcome landscapes of spiritual wilderness.

This means returning to the place of beholding and maintaining a beholding disposition even when it feels bland, unnecessary, unexciting, or unrevealing. In this posture of divine communion, we're dignifying God by allowing Him to be ungraspable, unattainable through all of it.

But our culture shapes our spirituality in other ways too, because we're constantly being consumed as products ourselves. So much so that you and I hardly notice it anymore. This has profound implications for our closeness with God. Every drive into the city is an opportunity for businesses to bombard us with thousands of little messages, all vying for our attention. Social media companies harvest minute details of our lives to offer specialised advertising packages to large corporations, and we presume it to be so normal that we don't think to challenge it anymore. We have become commodities. And the commodification of our beauty, goodness, and truth is just another reality in our new world.

The result? We come to assume that what God wants out of our time together is also productivity. Because if everyone around us, including organizations and even churches, use us for the value we add to them, and this is the way our entire world is structured, without serious consideration we'll make God in that same image. According to the rules of product-based consumerism, we will come to expect God to equate our value with the measure of our spiritual performance—be it total minutes of intercession clocked, spiritual gifts manifested, souls converted, or tears wept.

In that hubris, it doesn't even cross our minds that sitting with God and allowing Him to behold us could ever be a desire of His heart. And yet, God takes real and deep pleasure in us, even singing over us with joy and celebration.[6] God doesn't want to be consumed for what He offers us; He wants to be loved for Himself, and He repays us in kind, caring more for simply enjoying our presence than all the other stuff we think matters so much.

God Himself is no consumer.

There's a third element to this consumer worldview we inhabit. It's taught us to consume one another too. Our relationships run the danger of becoming about what we can get out of them and social events about how entertaining or satisfying we find them. If a gathering feels tiring or less worthy than simply staying at home, we avoid it. Including our Christian communities.

Other people, when they're exhausting us, when they're costing us, when they're different from us, or when they set us on edge, are marginalised in our lives as a result. If we can't learn to love God more than His gifts, and if we can't accept that we're loved by God as His own child rather than as His worker, then what hope do we have of really loving anyone else that way? Especially our enemies.

One of the methods this has worked its way out in the church is through pastors using congregants as a means to grow their ambitions. Churches have become places that launch book deals for talented pastors, print their own clothing labels, grow their social media base, or sell albums. It's painfully easy for members of church communities to translate into figures at staff meetings and for podcast-download numbers to equate to spiritual success.

The pastoral role in many places has become an opportunity for worldly fame and success.

And before you think I'm being judgemental here, I spent a decade as an artist in the Christian arena selling records and T-shirts and booking shows. I may not have been the lead pastor of a church, but I know personally how easy it is for the line to move and at other times how hard it is to even know what that line is. Even with the most sincere intentions.

One month Spotify numbers wouldn't bother me an iota, the next I could become obsessed. The challenge of gospel work in a consumer culture is profound, and I have by no means been immune. It takes awareness and commitment to swim against the tide of consumer Christianity; admitting it to ourselves may be hard, but it matters deeply.

On the other hand, it's also easy for members of church communities to consume their pastors for counseling, launching ministries, reconciliation meetings, or to achieve their own personal agendas, not in accompaniment to their own deep and difficult spiritual work, but in replacement of it. Consumerism is just as much about individuals *expecting* their pastors to be CEOs as it is church leaders wanting to be them.

I have many pastoral friends who have felt at times crushed by the unnecessary weight their congregants' expectations have placed on them. Our churches look like marketing agencies as much because we as individuals want them to as because of ambitious leaders. The sickness affects us all. Sadly, God can, and has, become a means for many of us in ministry to gain popularity, wealth, success, and personal significance. As I mentioned, I know from personal experience as a musician how it feels to oscillate between sincerity and ambition in the blurry Christian industry that occupies our times. Success is a powerful drug, even with the most genuine of hearts, and the current of our mainstream pop Christianity seems to tug us constantly toward its siren's call. It takes real resilience and focus to push back against it.

I've come to see my personal prayer time as the canary in the coal mine because when I stop sitting and waiting on God, and instead only pray when I need a "breakthrough," clarity on calling, or to alleviate my own sense of unworthiness for my own ambitions, I can be sure that I've slipped back into using the Kingdom for self-gain.

Our prayer relationship with God is essential. How this space holds is how all others will. Prayer matters.

Many of us feel all this consumer illness within us as an undiagnosed ache, and it's hard to acknowledge. But facing these challenges is our first step to healing.

For many raised in this milieu that constantly appeals to our emotional senses, this consumer spirituality is most notable in its pursuit of good feelings as the primary sign of God's presence. We often assume that the presence of these experiences equates to the Spirit moving, and that in their absence God must also be absent. However, feelings make great companions but terrible masters, and to use them as the watermark of the Spirit's activity in our lives runs the risk of our enthroning our emotions and becoming enslaved to them.

In our subconscious perception of God as a product to be consumed, we've learned to come to God for emotional satisfaction, mental relief, social transformation, spiritual power, or even worse, political endorsement. All of this (except the political endorsement part) can and should be the fruit of our being with God, but we slip out of beholding prayer and into consumer prayer when we judge how good our spiritual lives are based on how much we're getting from our time with God—from how much we *feel* it.

But God is mystery, so much more than our understanding and feelings can take hold of. It takes humility to approach Him. We have to let go of our assumptions, our needs for particular responses, and our preference for sense-making before belief. That's what faith is. It's our looking to God as good, and as a greater love, greater kindness, and greater compassion than we could ever understand. Even when we're not feeling it, or never have.

We can't force this Love to compete with our agendas, lists, complaints, or aggressive volume. We have to let God be as much a reality to us as gravitational force or the atoms that make up the world we inhabit are. We don't choose whether God is remarkable love or not; He simply is. Our doubting God's love can't make it untrue any more than my doubting the physics of flight would cause them to reverse. All we can do is accept it and let that truth transform us.

Love is patient, love is kind, love doesn't boast or force itself. God's voice is a whisper, and here we discover that love is heard less as the sound of a revival tent and more like the sound of breathing.

BEHOLDING, AN OPPOSITE WAY

There's an organic slow movement to beholding. It's a bit like relearning to breathe or to abide in the nuance of the year's seasonal changes. There's an essentiality to it that engulfs the rest of life. It can be many things in practice, but at its heart, it is the art of gazing at God. It's about sitting quietly for long enough to see who God really is and responding to the movements of His heart in that very time and space.

Beholding prayer is relentless in its passion for God alone, never bowing to ritual for ritual's sake or action as its first priority. It looks at God as the sole purpose of life, a spring of unending beauty, an inexhaustible object of adventure, joy, and celebration.

In beholding prayer, we don't get bored of God, because we have come to learn that every day we are different and as a result are able to see something different of Him. We come to see that whenever God feels learned or assumed, we're being invited into a new and exciting journey of discovering something about the real God behind our perceived image of Him. Prayer becomes inexhaustible because it draws from God's unending and complete goodness.

During the years when I couldn't work much because of my health, I noticed that I would run out of prayer fast, often before I

was ready to move on with my time. I had endless hours of nothingness in my days, and I desperately wanted to spend them with
God, taking the opportunity to meet with Him.

As I stayed with God beyond my agenda and formal prayers,
He began to show me things about the world and about life that
I didn't even have the imagination to ask. He started teaching
me His wisdom as a friend sitting with me on a deck during
sunset would. Communion became sharing our thoughts about
the world—philosophy, politics, family, church, history—and
we started to get to know what each other thought about all
that stuff.

That's what I mean by prayer becoming inexhaustible. God is
an endless source of wisdom, truth, and fascination. So often we
don't realise just how true that is because we don't stick around
long enough. I think we'd all be shocked to hear what God longs
to talk with us about if we just took a little more time to ask and
wait.

In that sense, communion with God can be very ordinary
because it involves our processing all parts of life with Him as we
go. We can behold God whilst we're washing the dishes, playing
with our children, or walking in nature. Beholding prayer is a disposition of openness to God in every moment because, whether
we see or feel Him there or not, He is there like oxygen. And we
know that wherever He is, He's there in His unchanging nature of
compassion, kindness, withness, and joy.

As retired Anglican Bishop Bruce Gilberd, a dear friend and
mentor, often says, "We must maintain a receiving disposition
toward God." That to me is the heart behind beholding prayer,

and it's a beautiful way of saying it. It's our creating space daily to awaken our awareness to Presence and to invite His gaze to be seen by ours. It's us, gazing at God, gazing at us.

We can do this simple act of acknowledgement in our cars before an appointment, in a meeting room during our lunch break, in bed when we're drinking our morning coffee, and at night with a candle before we sleep. None of this is about tiring ourselves out with words and agenda. If prayer is about asking and interceding alone, we'll spend time with God only when we have needs to pray about.

If words are our greatest asset, then we're bound to run out of things to say or to end prayer when our list does. But companionable silence is prophetic. It allows our conversations to begin on His terms. This way of being in the world is deeply countercultural. It goes against the flow of the entire Western mindset because we're so used to "taking hold" of our environments and lives. We're a very self-driven culture, and it seems to me, even in the church, we've forgotten that prayer is mostly the art of joining a conversation, not starting one.

Beholding prayer is a disposition of openness to
God in every moment because, whether we see or
feel Him there or not, He is there like oxygen.

Well before you or I even wake in the morning, God the Father, the Son, and the Spirit are conversing. They have been since well before the creation of the world and will continue well beyond its renewal. Prayer doesn't start when we sit down to close our eyes or when we think about it; it never ends, and so it makes perfect sense to me that we should come to God first of all as a listener-receiver: as a beholder. As someone who jumps into the divine river, rather than as someone who tries to create one by wringing out whatever energy they have within them.

That's what I mean by "companionable silence is prophetic," that the art of prophecy is really the art of listening, and the church is called to be a prophetic people. When we pray, when we open our minds and hearts toward God in any moment, we're simply joining the conversation.

BEING WITH GOD AMIDST OUR "WHYS"

Beholding, rather than consuming, God matures our under-standing of Him by allowing us to hold all kinds of tensions in our experience and understanding. It frees us from needing to understand God to know Him. It allows even suffering to coexist in our communion with Him, as the need for answers, though great, is no longer a prerequisite to Divine relating.

For years when my illness was peaking, I used to ask God, "Why?" Why wasn't He healing me, why was I sick in the first place, or what on earth was I sick with? But learning to behold changed that. As I learned to hold God's presence over personal closure, the question shifted from "Why am I sick?" to "Where are You amidst my suffering today?" Not because I was ignoring the pain I felt from God not healing me, but because it became less important in the face of my realising He was still there regardless.

"Why" demands understanding before communion. "Where" embraces communion before understanding; it invites a whole new conversation about the reality of God's immanence in every moment.

But there are other tensions, other "whys" too. "Whys" that *you* may feel more potently in your own life today. Why, if God loves me, am I still single? Why did He allow my child, marriage, or friend to die? Why has my life turned out this way when God promised me ...? Why, if God is close, can I not feel or hear Him? These are all important questions, and God doesn't want us to ignore them, but they're also questions that will swallow us up if they're prerequisites for divine communion. When we hold God above those questions, we allow His presence to envelop them and bring them calm. Beholding still believes God is worthy, still trusts He is good, and that in having Him we have everything we need for today.

Alternatively, consumer prayer denies God the space to simply be with us, or to challenge our preconceptions of Him because it defines God as a means to get what we want rather than as a means to an end in Himself. God becomes a static idea, an unmovable theology that serves our personal agendas rather than a revelatory Being inviting us deeper and deeper into a more complex and surprising understanding of Him. Consumer prayer stunts maturity.

When we first awaken to God, this simplistic view of Him is beneficial. We have to feel as though He is simple enough to touch, to have solid ideas about Him and the world, to receive from Him everything we want and need when we want and need it. We're like babies who depend on everything from their parents, from food to sleep to total emotional stability and routine.

But just like a parent with babies, God wants to grow us into deeper levels of complexity, understanding, and self-maturity, and if we're unable to discover this wider God beyond the God of our infancy, we can grow bored and lose the flame of devotional love. Because ultimately, a God who is totally consumable is not God at all, and deep down we thirst for the real living God.

Yet as we grow older, we can end up feeling like we've grown beyond Him somehow, like He's remained juvenile and we've become adults. We go looking for a better product in success, money, sex, or adventure. Or even worse, create a new god-product to consume that will only last another few years before a new model is needed again. No one is expected to relate to their parents at age twenty-one in the same way they did when they were two. So why should it be any different with the God of the universe?

Using God to get things done entirely relies on our presumption that we know what He wants to do. The problem with our very first understanding of God is its one-dimensional and simplistic view, much like when we were children. But as we grow in our faith, we need a way of praying that allows our understanding of God to grow and mature with us. This is what beholding prayer does. Like the parents who accept that their child who comes home after years of being away has actually changed and matured, so they treat their child almost like a new person, beholding prayer makes us malleable. By not assuming we have God tight knit, we keep our soul open and receptive to allow Him to be different for each of us.

For some, this consumption of God comes in the form of the God who blesses us when we do good things. For others, it's the God of judgement who is always on our side (or against us). For nations, God is the one who protects its borders and furthers its national political causes, and for another, it's the God who condones our behaviour with apathetic grace. These are only a few of the gods we come to know early in our faith, and the gods our generation is leaving behind as they grow, mature, and learn about the world.

These are the false gods we slay with the practice of beholding prayer.

You and I exist in a world that consumes—people, the environment, beauty, religion, and even God. Sadly, we can subconsciously come to see prayer similarly—as a place to get what we need from God, or to give God what He demands—and not as a place of divine pleasure and friendship. We are so used to a commodified economy that appreciating and admiring something beautiful without capitalising on it in some way takes real practice. It's an upside-down way of living.

Beholding is an invitation to this kind of counterculture. To relearn how to breathe. It's a way of being with God that doesn't demand emotional experiences, answers, or gifts as some kind of spiritual commodity, but just values God, however He longs to give Himself. Those things will come, because God is the most cheerful Giver, but they're not what satisfies us most. Our thirst can only be quenched by admiring and discovering the beauty, mystery, and love of God.

If consumerism is a way of seeing the world, then beholding is too. It's deeply transformative as a spiritual worldview. One that re-places value where it should be and, as a result, has a profound influence on how we move through our lives.

Chapter 3

A LOVE THAT CHANGES THINGS

"Jesus, help me to see what You saw, what You died for,
what the pain of crucifixion was worth for You—
the healing of this conversation between us."

Prayer Vol. 01

"Let me be among You.
Tangled up and engulfed by You;
on Your lap, against Your chest,
surrounded by the fragrance of You.
Satisfied and unsatisfied,
full and yet thirsty, overwhelmed
yet in peace with You....
I want to be among You,
As You are among You."

Prayer Vol. 02

"As the Father has loved me, so have I loved you."[7]

Jesus Christ

We were made for Love. He is the essence and driving force of all creation. There is no part of the world in which Love is not present, kindly and persistently inviting others to see, experience, and be transformed by Himself. Who on earth doesn't want love? The question isn't so much about whether it's wanted, but what kind we will choose to seek in our lives.

Jesus' answer to the question "What is the meaning of life?" is precisely that: love. When asked by a teacher of the law what the greatest commandment was, Jesus said, "'Love the Lord your God with all your heart and with all your soul and with all your mind.' This is the first and greatest commandment. And the second is like it: 'Love your neighbor as yourself.' All the Law and the Prophets hang on these two commandments."[8]

These are holy invitations, a blueprint for a flourishing human existence. We exist to give all our love to God, who is first giving it to us, and to allow that essential love to pour out over us into everyone and everything else.

So it goes without saying that love has always been the hope and centre of renewal in the Christian life; it has never left the church. But at times, the flame of love dims and it feels as though there is hardly enough oxygen left to keep it alive. We can feel stuck, looking at the church, holding our breath in the hope of just keeping the little of what's left alight. True love is a river that flows downstream to us from the heart of God, so a lack of love could be diagnosed as a lack of sitting in the river of God Himself. True love and prayer are inseparable realities.

The church has never stopped praying, and yet there are seasons when it feels like all our prayer has contributed little to our patience, kindness, gentleness, self-control, and compassion as a people. We may be seeing the gifts of God—missional objectives, charismatic pastors, growing church attendance, even physical miracles—but we're seeing very little of the fruit: the peacemaking, humility, and meekness that Christ promised would embody His New World.

You can tell a lot about the values of a people by looking at their living heroes, and these days ours are often more the embodiment of consumer culture than the antithesis of it. That may have felt sufficient to some in more moderate times, but in the divisive world of our today, people are at least as starved for acceptance, kindness, and love as they are for charismatic sermons, healing, and miracles.

In my early twenties I spent a lot of time around Pentecostal communities. I was engrossed by meetings where masses would fall over in the Spirit, speak in other languages, and have visions and experiences that you'd only read of in books. I loved it. But I started to notice an unfortunate reality about the traveling power evangelists who led those meetings and many of the leaders in those communities. Those same people, when they weren't on stage performing great spiritual wonders, were often brittle, agitated, self-ambitious, and unkind.

The same ambition that made them able to fast for forty days and go on extensive missions could also make them relational steamrollers. Of course, we're all broken humans, and evangelists and traveling preachers are no different. But this was more of a pattern than an aberration. A desire for spiritual power leading to the overuse of natural power. In reality, demonstrating God's power doesn't necessarily equate to a gentle and loving person.

I never lost my desire for seeing God move miraculously, and I'm in no way cynical about vibrant Pentecostal communities (I love them!), but I knew then that those works of God weren't worth the cost of love. Demonstrations of God are hollow without the nature of God.

I'm not picking on Pentecostalism either, because it's just as true of commercially structured churches with CEO pastors who are great at running the organisation of the church community but who aren't gentle, praying people. It's also true of those given passionately to social justice issues who become self-righteous and harsh as their frustration grows at the lack of progress they see in the world. All created light casts its shadow. The fruit of love is a far more precious resource than the giftedness of man.

In those years, my early twenties, when I was bursting into my faith with a burning-hot first fervour, many of my friends and I wanted to see the miracles of the New Testament. I still do. But as the years have passed and that first fervour has given birth to a deeper and more persistent and admiring second love, I've come to see that kindness is a miracle, self-control a shocking characteristic, gentleness and humility rare commodities, and Christian unity almost worthy of greater awe than dead-raising. We were looking for the "grand" stuff, but surprisingly, the "little" stuff was harder to come by.

In the end, it wasn't for a lack of charisma and miracles that many of my peers left the faith; it was their pain and shock at the rarity of these humble fruits of the Spirit in the leaders and communities they belonged to. They left because they were longing for a love that actually changes things, changes people, and they didn't feel like they were finding it in their churches. Miracles, gifted experiences, and charismatic personalities, as it turns out, aren't enough.

FLOATING AND CANOEING IN THE RIVER OF GOD

But why, when we've not stopped praying and worshipping, has this kind of Christlikeness become so rare?

Maybe it's because it's *how* we're praying, not just *that* we're praying, that we need to consider. If God is a river of love, ever moving us deeper in the direction of His heart, then we could imagine prayer as both floating and canoeing. Canoeing could be thought of as our intercession, petition, and praise, the kind of prayer that opens the veil for God's movement in the world in which we live. Moving through the river like this takes some arm work and energy on our part. It's involved and proactive.

But there's a floating kind of prayer too, the sort where we're belly up, like leaves at the mercy of the currents and eddies of the water. It's restful prayer, prayer that helps us to become one with the river in a profound way. For some, canoeing is easier; for others, it's floating. A healthy life of communion needs both floating (or abiding, as Jesus calls it) and paddling (intercession, petition, and the gifts).

As we've seen, the consumer society we inhabit has formed us far more as paddlers—largely doing prayers—and, as a result, so much of what we consider mature prayer is in the realm of petition, repentance, and intercession. But just paddling away with

God without a healthy dose of floating on the river, gazing up at the clouds drifting by, and enjoying the sounds and hues of green along the water's edge can wear us out, and we can soon forget why we're on the journey in the first place. It can also lead to spiritual assumption, because if we're not spending enough time in God's love, our assumptions about what that love is remain purely theoretical.

The fruit of love is a far more precious resource than the giftedness of man.

This, in part I believe, has contributed to an expression of love centred primarily on vocal protest. This is a shadow kind of prophetic orientation that cuts away at things with a moral machete, imagining that bringing something down, or cancelling it, is justice and building a better world. Our generation places an emphasis on opinion, on voice, and on the importance of being right. It's good to be strong in the truth. But speaking the truth is not the same as being loving—not in a godly sense.

We can become strong on truth but weak on speaking and living it with an attractive tenderness and empathy. We can have the right words but not the right nature—the Christ nature—and the latter is much harder to obtain. Believing truth is easy; appropriating it is hard, one might even say impossible, without God.

It's easy to see why we've become so fixated on being right when the world has become significantly noisier through globalisation, the hyper connection of the internet, and especially social media. Opinions that were once confined to the number of friends we had are now aired on digital platforms with the potential to reach millions. In the face of the opinion wars and overuse of technology of our times, many of us are living in perpetual thinness, short, dry matches prone to being lit any moment in a love-droughted world by someone else's opposing statements.

Technology overuse is a great thief of abiding, and it's become a cultural norm. The danger is that technology overuse empties our reservoir for empathy and considerate conversation whilst simultaneously offering us an immediate platform to express our thin, emotional responses. A self-perpetuating cycle then leads to greater and greater escalation, which is something we've begun to see the tip of in the present political crises and global erosion of truth.

It's an easy win being right too, in a religious sense. Often, study is easier than prayer. The fight for justice is easier than self-reflection and repentance. We can hide behind good religious activities by focusing on our doing *for* God without our being *with* Him. Throw into the mix undercurrents of political conspiracies and the bottomless YouTube pit, and we can quickly be led to believing that our seeking and promulgating what we believe is "the truth" are the same thing as following and abiding in Jesus. Being right does not equal being righteous. We need

Christ for that, and He's a person long before He is an ideology or a movement.

But true prophetic voices spring up out of a well of kindness, their pinch coming not from anger or irritability but from their patient and compassionate resolve. That's how Christ did it, if we're to hold Him to the fruits His Spirit bears. Jesus didn't come to condemn the world, but to save it. That means something. His words of life and invitation followed Him in every street throughout Israel as He healed, welcomed strangers, and opposed nonloving theologies and social structures in the very fruits of the Spirit we find in Galatians.

If we are to be a unifying, welcoming prophetic presence in our disconnected world, we're going to need to discover *that* kind of prophetic temperament. And it's not going to be appropriated through textbooks.

That's why I believe we can say, as we already have, that whenever we see a weakness of love in the church, we can diagnose it first as a weakness of prayer. And not just any prayer, but floating prayer. Because prayer, or divine communion, is where love is learned, or better said, known.

Prayer is the abiding in the God of love we were called to in the Garden. It's so much more than petition and intercession; it's communion, an invitation to sit with God and to learn what He looks, feels, and sounds like. When prayer is whittled down to practicality and function, so are our fundamental beliefs about relationships. So is our theology. So is our God.

If prayer is fundamentally about intercession and petition, then it is fundamentally about working *with* God. This form of prayer is magnificent, and Christ calls us to it, but without the balance of devotion *to* God, it can look like godly action without godly nature. Gifts without the fruit. Truth without love.

When I was younger, I worked for my parents in their consulting business. During the days, my father was my boss and that meant we dialogued over objectives and key performance indicators. But outside of work hours, we left all that behind because it was secondary to our relationship as father and son. Yes, I worked for my dad, but that wasn't what defined our relationship. And so it is with God.

When it comes to balancing *doing* prayer and *being* prayer, or canoeing and floating, it's exactly the same. Yes, we work for and with God but always as the secondary context to our holy friendship. Of course, we learn things on the go, and working together is still a relationship, but it takes spending time with God as family, receiving from Him, hearing His words, and learning His temperament to become like Him. And it's in our becoming like Him that our truth embodies love.

All intercession and petition and no beholding and abiding makes only half a relationship with God, and as far as our friendship goes, not the most important half.

BECOMING FRIENDS WITH GOD

I've not met a Christian in all the world who would contest that God is love, and yet the truth is, many of us struggle with transforming the theology of divine love into something concrete. Something that actually changes how we feel and think when we wake up in the morning. It's one thing to sit and hear a sermon about how God loves us no matter what, but it's another thing entirely to appropriate that truth amidst our failure, unbelief, shame, or just the ordinary day-to-day work and responsibilities that inhabit the majority of our lives.

In order to receive the kind of love that actually changes things, we need to do two things: we need to move from a transactional gospel to a familial one, and we need to practise receiving from God as much as we ask or give.

How do we move from a transactional to familial gospel? Well, it starts with what we believe the purpose of Christ's incarnation, death, and resurrection really was. Many of us have been taught, or often subtly believe, that the main purpose for Christ's death and resurrection was forgiveness. We could call this the transactional gospel; we had a debt to pay, and God sent His Son to pay it for us.

In this gospel our relationship with God is about keeping the sin balance sheet at zero through repentance, praying for others to repent, and thanking God for forgiving us when we do. Here we see Christ on the cross suffering for our sin so we wouldn't need to go to hell anymore, and in turn, our lives are about utilising that sacrifice to clear the slate every time we sin. It's a sin-focused gospel.

Now I want to be careful here, because of course the Scriptures do tell us that Jesus died for our sins, and hallelujah for that! But they're also clear that this wasn't the main reason He came. Just as while I was working for my dad you would be right in calling me his employee but would be more right in calling me his son, we're right in saying that Jesus dealt with our sin through the cross, but that this isn't the greater truth of the matter either. It wasn't His ultimate goal.

His ultimate goal was that He would make Himself radically available to us for closeness once more. Or in the New Testament language, Christ came for "reconciliation" as we read in 2 Corinthians 5:16–20:

> So from now on we regard no one from a worldly point of view. Though we once regarded Christ in this way, we do so no longer. Therefore, if anyone is in Christ, the new creation has come: The old has gone, the new is here! All this is from God, who reconciled us to himself through Christ and gave us the ministry of reconciliation: that God was reconciling the world to himself in Christ, not counting people's sins against them. And he has committed to us the message of reconciliation. We are therefore Christ's ambassadors, as though God were making his appeal through us. We implore you on Christ's behalf: Be reconciled to God.

Forgiveness wasn't Christ's ultimate goal on the cross. Reconciliation was. And there's an important difference. Reconciliation literally means the restoration of friendship. This is profound, and it changes everything about the way we pray.

Classically, to forgive someone is simply to clear their debt. Forgiveness doesn't demand any more than that. It clears another's record so that they can move on without judgement and condemnation, but it says nothing of the quality or type of life that is to be lived beyond it. Especially when it comes to their relationship with the forgiver.

I can forgive my children after they smash a window inside playing ball by not punishing them, but that's not the same thing as staying close and tender toward them afterwards. I may not punish them, but without friendship and a restoration to my softness afterwards, how will they know that I still love or like them? It's not the consequences my children fear most; it's my detachment from them. The loss of unconditional closeness.

Forgiveness is a profound act of grace and kindness; it says, "I will no longer punish you for your hurtful actions," but it has nothing more to offer after that.

So many of us are like children who feel as though God has forgiven us but that He doesn't like us. All we've been taught is that Jesus *had* to die for us, and now we have some kind of legal right to claim His name whenever we haven't measured up.

However, that gospel doesn't tell us if God's happy with us or not. Whether His heart swells with joy every time we lock eyes with Him, or whether He wants to sit together after dinner for a heart to heart. It's entirely possible to believe you're forgiven but not that you're liked. If that's how we feel, then prayer, even after receiving the good news of Christ, remains savaged by the need to earn God's approval.

A transactional gospel like this leads to transactional prayer. Prayer centred on giving and taking, be it forgiveness or approval. It's our worshipping Him so we might receive His presence. Repenting so we can be lovable. Interceding so we can be effective.

In transactional prayer, we don't pray *from* acceptance but *for* it. Nor out of desire, but duty. Prayer is like a tally; we give more so we can receive more back. But often out of scarcity, not devotion. It's friendshipless, or beingless, prayer.

Equally painful, a transactional gospel can lead our preaching to become all about sin or about what God is asking us to do for Him. Because if forgiveness is the pinnacle of the gospel, then behavior modification, mission, and repentance are the most important threads. Without the call to climb higher into the adventure of divine friendship, our preaching lacks the wonder, beauty, and celebration the kingdom of heaven is truly meant to be. We run the risk of becoming a bad taste in the mouth of the world. All broken bread, no wine.

Sometimes I wonder if this is all the world has seen or learned from us over the years: a transactional spirituality more obsessed with the evil in the world and our personal sin than with the wonder of divine friendship that God's love came to give us.

If the cross, and Christ's life, was only about forgiveness, then where do we go once we've confessed, repented, and interceded? Prayer becomes limited to as much of that as we can think of. Anything else feels superfluous, self-gratifying, or "navel gazing" as some call it. Forgiveness offers us no vitality in our relationship with God beyond working for or with Him. It's no wonder so many struggle to pray in a relational and loving way with God when they believe He's so sin obsessed. Sin was a barrier to overcome in order to reconcile us *to* something. But that was never the end.

Thank God that's not the whole gospel! Because reconciliation, on the other hand, is an invitation into the completely uncharted territory of sharing life with and exploring the magnitude of the loving God. It doesn't just say, "Okay, things are right between us now; you can move on with your life without debt."

Reconciliation says, "Forget what you owe Me; I want you, I want what we had before this crisis, I want your presence in its fullness being fully enjoyed by Me as I'm fully enjoyed by you. I've sorted what's owed; forget that. Now you can truly know, feel, and experience how much I love and celebrate you, and you can know Me as that Father again."

Forgiveness takes us back to the fall, to mend a terrible mistake that led to a history of hate, violence, and fear. But reconciliation takes us further back still, to creation, where we woke from the dust of the earth face to face with God as we inhaled His breath, becoming human. In that moment of our existence, in its most unadulterated form, all we had was to stare into the eyes of God forever and discover Him.

It's entirely possible to believe you're forgiven but not that you're liked. If that's how we feel, then prayer, even after receiving the good news of Christ, remains savaged by the need to earn God's approval.

This is the birth story of communion, and of beholding prayer. Yes, it's imperative that we acknowledge that we sin and, even worse, that we're sinners. Our sin has distorted creation and harmed many billions of lives. There can be no true communion, no real beholding without acknowledging that painful truth first. But to leave it there, or to assume that fixing the sin issue that followed this original expression of communion was Christ's end on the cross, is to belittle God's deep desire for world-altering love.

This is the gospel, and how incredible it is. That God hasn't just forgiven us; He's fully restored our place at His table of friendship forever. It is stunning that we might be called friends of God, and it transforms the way we see prayer entirely.

EXPERIENCING GOD'S LOVE IN OUR BEING

But how do we meaningfully land this as an experience within ourselves? How can this become a love that actually changes things and not just another heady theological affirmation? I spent close to a decade knowing that God loves me without it being a dwelling reality within me, and when I started to get more and more sick, the ache for that to change only got more powerful.

When I go back and read through over ten years of journaling during that time, one theme persists with a deep kind of pain: the need for God to show me that He actually loves me. I knew it in my mind, but I couldn't feel it in my soul, and I knew that it was stopping me from knowing Him. It wasn't until I finally started the prayerful practice of acceptance that things began to change for me.

I remember the morning God confronted me with the strange fact that I had been rejecting His love all the time that I had been asking for it. My second son was a bad sleeper, and he would often wake up anywhere between 3 and 4.30 am for the day. Most of my prayer during those years was just me sitting in bed with my coffee, a good dose of extreme brain fog, and a desire to make the most of my time with God.

Prayer for years had felt like my reaching up and out to someone, trying to pull Him in, and that's what I was doing that morning. I was asking God to manifest His love to me when He snapped me out of it with this invitation. In the middle of my aching request, the Spirit gently interrupted, saying, "Strahan, stop asking Me to show you My love, and just accept it."

Suddenly, scriptures started coming to mind of His promises of love toward me. Scriptures like, "As the Father loved me, I too have loved you," "And surely I am with you always, to the very end of the age," "God's love has been poured out into our hearts through the Holy Spirit, who has been given to us," and "The LORD your God is with you … He will take great delight in you; in his love he will no longer rebuke you, but will rejoice over you with singing."[9]

But as much or even greater than all those scriptures He reminded me of is the one simple truth that He *is* love.[10] That to be in His presence at all is to be in the presence of pure unadulterated love. Because God is ever-giving love, it's impossible to have Him without it. He doesn't love us only by choice but by nature. There is no Spirit without it. And we know what that love feels like; it feels like peace, patience, joy, kindness, and gentleness.[11] To stand before or to be in or indwelt by God is to have no choice but to be wrapped up in all this goodness.

That morning I realised I'd spent over a decade desperately seeking a love I refused to acknowledge I already had. I had come up with all kinds of excuses for why I personally couldn't receive love as an action—personal sin, failure, inability to feel it, mental struggle, not holy enough—but now I was seeing that as much as I used those self-defeating reasons not to receive the action of love, I was also accidentally ignoring the Person of love. There is simply no God without love. He can't help Himself.

Instead of seeking something I didn't have that day ... instead of trying to understand it, or finding a reason to believe it, or waiting for it to hit me from above, I simply closed my eyes and connected my imagination with reality. I laid my palms open before me, and I said, "Father, You are inexhaustible and magnificent love. I believe that You're within me, that You love being here, and that You are radiating Yourself through every part of my being as You promised."

Then I welcomed that belief into my bones. Not only my mind and my rationale, but into my very being.

Prayer like this takes time to truly transform a life. I wish I could say it all changed for me that one morning, but it didn't. Morning by morning and day by day, I kept coming back to that kind of prayer—receiving prayer—and I still do. I spent sometimes hours whilst I was sick during those months and years simply sitting in silence, allowing God to love me, allowing my mind and body to inhabit it. And slowly it did. Slowly, it began to feel like I could move more and more quickly into its possession in times of fear, shame, or anxiety.

I had been asking for Love my whole life, expecting it to come at me from heaven in some kind of tangible, miraculous way. Instead, I needed to awaken to the reality of its existence within me. To accept it not as something God gives, but as who He is. I needed to commit myself to daily sitting in that reality and nothing else, welcoming, believing, receiving, and experiencing it.

It was through this realisation that I noticed my own nature changing. I began to see others differently, to treat my children with more patience. I became a little slower, a little less angry, a little less anxious. I was learning that the greatest power in prayer is to *be* together with God and that being is often as much the answer to the prayers we're praying as the answers we're seeking themselves.

Jesus promised the way to this love is not complicated or for the initiated. Standing in the public space during a festive gathering of the people of Israel, He declared this profound open invitation: "Let anyone who is thirsty come to me and drink. Whoever believes in me, as Scripture has said, rivers of living water will flow from within them."[12]

We're called primarily to come and drink from God, not to come and think. Not in an anti-intellectual way, but with a posture that makes thirst personal, not theoretical. One hydrates, illuminates, and energises our love through the act of receiving; the other works and strives with the mind in an attempt to attain it. Anyone who has tried to sit a school exam dehydrated will tell you about the futility of thinking without drinking. Clarity of mind comes through drinking water. We can't think our way to hydration. So it is with God.

Love is the meaning of life and more specifically receiving, participating, and sharing God's love with others. A Love that doesn't just right wrongs but restores wrongdoers to friendship and joy with Himself. Without this kind of love, truth is tasteless and weaponised. It may be right, but not righteous.

There is simply no God without
love. He can't help Himself.

But we also need to open ourselves up to it, to accept it. It has to be a love that actually changes things, and for that to happen, it must be welcomed into our being. We must say, "Yes, Father, I trust You; I know You love me," and to spend time daily allowing that reality to inhabit our being. We must allow ourselves to be truly beheld by God as objects of His affection and to let that transform us.

Communion is wonderfully simple. To discover Love all we need to do is quietly come to Him. To invite the Holy Spirit and, with a contrite heart and a humble way about us, sit and wait. Not just once, or even twice, but over and over again for the rest of our living days. The question isn't "Does God love us?" but whether we'll allow the fact that He always does to become an experienced reality in our daily lives.

Chapter 4

THE DIVINE HONGI

"Father,
teach me presentness,
as prayer."

Prayer Vol. 02

"On that day you will realize that I am in my Father,
and you are in me, and I am in you."[13]

Jesus Christ

"Pray without ceasing."[14]

St Paul the Apostle

In the beginning, when there is only silence and void, God creates. Like Bach, Mozart, or Beethoven, He weaves threads of life, gravity, and the suspense of spring and autumn with profound pleasure and promise. Explosions of life spring up into the vacuum of space. Twisted rock and gas, galaxies of dust and debris form a cosmos stretching so far it bends the tracks of time itself.

There amidst everything, a marble of green and blue is suspended. Sea and land separate with the clap of God's hands, earth and sky pull apart by His joy-filled laughter. Life pops up in all kinds of species and places.

But it isn't enough. God has something else on His mind. A deeper, more fulfilling relationship that can't yet be found in any other thing He's made. His love wants to be shared; He wants to create something that can return to Him the vivacious joy He feels and can commune free of all the kinds of instincts or laws the rest of creation is bound by.

So God kneels down on the musty soil of planet Earth and begins to gather it up into clumps. Tears of joy and love roll from His eyes, softening the dirt, giving Him workable substance to bring into form a wonder unseen in the cosmos till then. Hands ... feet ... a head to carry the mind ... a heart to inhabit the chest. Legs, fingers, eyebrows, and organs. God makes His human.

Next, so He can guarantee the image of this new creature will reflect His own, He does something exceptional. He leans over and kneels beside the form, laying out His legs and knees over ours, His chest against our chest, His arms stretched outward across our arms until His face is finally pressed up against ours. Then, from His abundant longing, He takes a deep, excited breath and breathes out His life force.

Our lungs expand, and we take our very first breath. Out of complete darkness we awaken to life as a cosmic infant, not even knowing yet how to open our eyes. Slowly, we draw up the muscles above our eyebrows, prying open our eyelids.

In this sacred moment, this first impression of what life and the world will be, the very first thing we see is not the soil, vast emptiness, or even a garden; it's the face of God. Eye to eye, mouth to mouth, chest to chest.

This very first vision we're shown of us and God in those first pages of Genesis is of a profound intimacy. Of a continuous consciousness of God. Of a Divine Hongi.

The hongi is a tradition among Māori here in Aotearoa, New Zealand that speaks to me of the profound moment of creation between God and us in the very beginning.

The hongi is the gentle pressing of noses together in which one another's breath—our "ha" or life force—is intermingled.[15] Usually, during a hongi, you'll shake hands with one arm and embrace the shoulder of the other person in a loose hug. It's a full body experience in which for a good moment of time, two people occupy one space. My friend Bradford Haami, current chair of Te Rūnanga o te Wānanga Amorangi (The Māori Council for Christian Theological School Laidlaw College), told me that Māori traditionally used to recount their ancestry together during the hongi until they found a common ancestor to unite them. What a powerful experience that must have been.

The hongi is a moment of togetherness, "a sign of peace and also a sign of life and well-being," according to Māori, that can bring "oneness of thought, purpose, desire, and hope."[16] It's an hospitable act. It's also confronting and overwhelming for those unaccustomed to it.

Many of us aren't used to being this close to people we hardly know; we're prone to a highly individualised and personal space-keeping way of living. At best we've come to expect a more transactional-based relationship with those we've never met before, keeping them at arm's distance socially until we've got to know them better. But the shock of the hongi is what makes it feel so holy to participate in.

I'm Pākehā (a non-Māori New Zealander), but the hongi, which I've received from friends and strangers, both in and out of a marae context (*marae* is an important communal and sacred place for Māori) has been a real gift to my understanding not only of human connection but of my own relationship to God. I can't think of anything in my own culture as someone of European descent quite like it. The hongi invites me to see relationship as something totally engulfing with God, a "bare all to be one" kind of friendship.

Likewise, in Genesis when God creates us, we don't just wake up somewhere alone, wondering what to do and how to make sense of the world ourselves. We wake up in direct contact with our Maker. In hongi.

We could have met with God any way that first moment between us. We could have been delivered a contract; He could have been sitting across from us ready to explain the situation logically. But instead, God crosses the spiritual divide and we awake to receive a life-giving embrace from the Creator of this miraculous world. We're welcomed not only into proximity with God, but into the closest form of contact, sharing our life forces together.

We awaken to seeing the world through His eyes, face to face, skin close and full of His breath. Our coming to existence was about a God-confronted life in which our experience of the world, ourselves, and of our Maker was unified. Our first impression of life being this deep sharing of "purpose, desire, and hope."

The hongi is powerful because it changes the nature of the relationship between two people. Not like a contract, in the formal way of Western commercial culture, but in the deeply personal form of giving our own life force to another to create something bigger than both of us—a shared life.

That's what prayer is—a dynamic conversation between us and God spoken in our very life.

As I came to realise I was leaving behind a working relationship with God for a friendship, and discovered this beholding kind of existence with Him, this moment in our Genesis origin story started to transform my understanding of what it means to be human.

The idea of living in continual hongi with God becoming the way I understood what it means to pray ceaselessly.

But there's a deeper invitation still to be found in the image of the hongi. If you're visiting a marae, a crucial part of the welcoming ceremony is being received this way by the hosts. Before receiving the hongi, visitors are considered just that, visitors. But afterwards, "manuhiri [visitors] are now tangata whenua [people of the marae] for the duration of their stay."[17]

We're welcomed as friends.

As Pākehā, to be not only invited to share sacred space with the local *iwi* (tribe), but to be considered, even temporarily, as one of their own in some way, is humbling and confronting. My ancestors considered land a property to own and defend, but through their generosity and humility, Māori have inspired me to see myself as more of a custodian rather than an owner of whatever land I occupy or travel across, making me more attentive to care for creation and to be welcoming of strangers.

Sadly, Pākehā came to abuse this sacred invitation, using it not to honour Māori but to excuse colonisation and land grabbing. Since the Garden, where we also misused God's vulnerable and open invitation, humanity has been taking rather than giving. A behaviour painfully evident in the history of colonisation in Aotearoa. But the hongi is an invitation into mutually dignifying vulnerability, not an invitation to overrun, assimilate, or take advantage of another.

When I think of Genesis through this notion of invitation into sacred space, it takes on a whole new dimension. There, we see a similar, holy-sharing taking place. God has created the world; it's His and He has dominion over it. We could imagine it as His marae. So that not only was God inviting us into Himself, but He was also welcoming us into His place as one of His own. As a people who belong to a world enchanted and made to be a communion table between Him and us.

We're welcomed not only into proximity with
God, but into the closest form of contact,
sharing our life forces together.

That doesn't mean we can treat it however we like, or that it doesn't remain God's holy space. But it does mean we're invited to come and eat with God and participate in His creative activity in the world. We were soil when God breathed life into us. To live right with God is to live right with creation.

The idea of the Divine Hongi is an invitation to unceasing prayer and to a reconciled life, a beyond transactional one. It's an invitation to a new way of existence, and a new way of understanding what being with God really means for our moving through the world.

I needed this paradigm shift in my understanding of prayer, because I'd always understood my relationship with God far more contractually, tit-for-tat. Even when I thought about my being

God's child, I thought of it as something God "purchased" or "paid for," and therefore prayer was often an oscillation between connection and disconnection.

But what the Divine Hongi invites me into is far more up close and embedded. It tells a different story about what Christ came for—my learning to live life intermingled with God.

This life together isn't aethereal and untouchable either, because in the hongi we see the meeting place of humanity, God and the earth. This hongi is embodied; it's about meeting God through ourselves and through our connection to the land. There's a redemptive tone in there for everything we do, linking our relationship to creation, each other, and God together in a profound way. To participate in the hongi of Genesis, we must also hongi one another, we must also hongi the physical world we inhabit.

Sadly, our Garden story didn't end there. We chose to look away from the Divine Hongi. To behold the world not through God's eyes, but our own. We turned our gaze inward, to ourselves and our own desires, and in turning away, we felt the pain of losing this intimacy with our Maker.

Which makes what Jesus did with His disciples between His resurrection and Pentecost so deeply profound. As we read in John 20:21–22:

> Again Jesus said, "Peace be with you! As the
> Father has sent me, I am sending you." And with
> that he breathed on them and said, "Receive the
> Holy Spirit."

Jesus, alone with His followers in a room that day, restored us to Divine Hongi. He didn't just come to square off some kind of holy balance sheet. He wasn't just here to show us a new way of life or teach us how to be better people. The gospel is far grander than that. It's more personal, more confronting.

To a Hebrew mind for whom the creation narrative was memorized and paramount, this was an eye-watering moment. There, in that room, God was saying, "Welcome home." Not only to acceptance by God, but to a beautiful, shared life. To a new experience of creation. To the oldest covenant restored. To Divine Hongi.

This is what the New Testament is talking about when it declares to us that we're *reconciled* to God. Remember, the gospel is about so much more than sin; it's about friendship, and the kind of friendship we're told we're being restored to is the hongi-close kind.

When God first breathed life into us, that breath stayed. It wasn't a once off; His breath became the very thing that has sustained our life for many millennia since. Now, Jesus gives us His breath again, His resurrected, post-cross breath, and this too is far more than a temporary offering. It's an invitation into the continuous life of God again in a new way.

Only a few days after Jesus breathed on His disciples, Pentecost came, and an even more profound intimacy than Genesis was revealed. In this new covenant, the Divine Hongi isn't just a face-to-faceness like the Garden; it's our welcoming into the Trinitarian life itself. This hongi didn't just invite us into God's creation with Him, it invited us into God Himself, and His being homed within our very bodies.

CLOSING THE GAP BETWEEN
THEOLOGY AND EXPERIENCE

But faith and prayer don't always feel this way, do they? We can often feel that despite a few moments of real encounter with God, where He feels as real as the skin on our bodies, we spend most of our lives looking outward for God, trying to find Him. We can feel as though prayer is about pulling God into our lives because He feels absent. This reality I'm talking about seems reserved for "spiritual" folk somewhere else. The theology of intimacy with God and the idea of Divine Hongi are beautiful to imagine, but what other practices can help us live into them?

I have to confess, I don't remember much about my wedding day. I remember Katie walking down the aisle toward me and feeling a deep sense of knowing that this was the best decision I'd ever made. A feeling of wonder.

Unfortunately for me, I also remember the DJ having to restart our first-dance track three times because I kept forgetting the routine we'd spent two months practising to wow our friends (I'm not sure anyone else forgot that either!). But I was so painfully nervous about the logistics of the day that everything else turned to a blur.

What I do know, however, is this: that day when Katie and I made a covenant to be together for the rest of our lives, it was the beginning of a journey, not the fulfilment of it. We needed to live into it, and still do. Every day that we're together sharing the road, loving each other, and going through the highs and lows of life, we're making our marriage truer.

And yet, we can also honestly say that from that blurringly magnificent day on, we were married, proper. Our marriage was complete that day, and we've been making it more complete ever since.

Living with God is the same. At baptism we're filled with the Spirit and, in turn, the fullness of God. We're *married*, we might say. But that marriage, that salvation, doesn't just finish there; it needs to be lived out. Our fully "having" God needs to live its way into every area of our lives and through every season.

Salvation, or the Divine Hongi, isn't a static reality. It's a living, breathing relationship. An organic thing. We might even say it's the kind of living Paul spoke of when he encouraged us to "pray without ceasing."[18]

For our Christian forebears, this leaning into what we already have and making it more true was the purpose of spiritual practices. Not primarily "things we need to do to be saved" or tools for becoming a better person, but as the day-to-day out-working of the invitation to the God-soaked life. To living into the Divine Hongi.

The theological reality of God's withness, like any other relationship, needs to be welcomed into our lives, bodies, and minds. As we do that, what is true becomes more true and our friendship with God deepens.

That's prayer.

Early in the life of the church, devoted saints noticed this very thing. They could tell, though we're full to the brim with God, we don't seem to move or live or sense life as if that's the case. The Divine Hongi may be our theological reality, but our felt experience seems at odds with it.

The saints saw that we need to awaken ourselves to it somehow. So, around the fifth century in Egypt, some Desert Fathers developed a simple and powerful way to do exactly that, and they called it the Jesus Prayer.

A "HONGI" PRAYER

The Jesus Prayer is simple and short, "Lord Jesus Christ, Son of God, have mercy on me," with some adding "a sinner" on the end. It's a combination of two prayers in the gospel: the blind man on the road who cried "Jesus, Son of David, have mercy on me!" and the publican in Jesus' parable who "would not even lift up his eyes to heaven … saying, 'God, be merciful to me, a sinner!'"[19] It was meant to be repeated during particular prayer times and then throughout the day as a way of invoking God's presence.

The Jesus Prayer isn't meant to be babbled away as a mental exercise; it's much more intentional than that. St Nicodemus, an eighteenth-century monk, theologian, and philosopher talked about the prayer in this way:

> Prayer of the heart ... consists primarily of a person placing his mind within the heart and, without speaking with his mouth, but only with inner words spoken in the heart, saying this brief and single prayer: "Lord Jesus Christ, Son of God, have mercy on me."[20]

To place your mind within your heart and then to speak without words. What a definition for prayer! To bring the mind into the heart doesn't mean to pray emotionally, necessarily. For the early church the heart was the seat of the interior life, not just feelings. When we bring our minds down into our hearts, we're seeing prayer not only as an intellectual exercise—a place to transfer information—but as a loving one.

It's to be present to God and ourselves, to the words we're saying, to how we're expressing ourselves to Him. It's about intentionality.

In our hyper-world, we're not used to being fully present to our bodies, so to pray this way can be a much-needed counterbalance. If we struggle to get out of our heads and move down into our hearts, we can start by noticing our surroundings. What are the sounds, smells, feelings, or colours around us? How do our bodies feel? Where can we feel our bodies connecting with our seats or the ground beneath us? As we do this, we begin to reattach our *headiness* to our *bodiness* which in turn helps us pray with our whole being.

The end goal is then bringing all of this being to God and to pray from there. Bringing our minds down into our hearts is a bit like focusing during a conversation with a friend. Sometimes our minds can wander whilst another is talking. But if that person begins sharing about something deep, painful, or important, and we realise they need more than just head nods and half-present smiles, we pause internally for a moment and try to sink into it more, listening with all of ourselves. We respond with a deeper look, empathetic body language, and eyes of intent. We listen with all of ourselves.

To place your mind within your heart and then to speak without words. What a definition for prayer!

Before, we could hear them, but we weren't listening. Now, we're engaging all our empathy, attentiveness, and care even though all the inner distractions might beckon us still. So it goes with prayer. Sometimes we can be rattling off words or listening to God halfheartedly because we're all mindy. Taking a moment to lock in, focus our minds into our hearts, and pray with soulful meaning is when true prayer begins.

The Jesus Prayer is a way that millions have practised making this a reality in their lives.

When we pray in that way, we're uniting our bodies in prayer with God and sinking into the reality that He lives within us. We're also inviting Him to pour Himself ever more into us as we live our lives. It's not an intellectual exercise; it's an experiential disposition.

The word "mercy" here isn't what most of us think it is either. It's not so much about forgiveness and repentance. The word "mercy" here is more of an invitation to God for His love, as author Frederica Mathewes-Green put it in her book *The Illumined Heart*:

> Mercy is slightly different [to forgiveness]. The
> Hebrew word is *hesed*, meaning "steadfast love," a
> love that perseveres to save the beloved. In Greek
> it's *eleos*, and "Lord, have mercy" is *Kyrie, elei-*
> *son*. In that language it resonates poetically with
> *elaion*, olive oil, the medium for medicinal balm.
> The Good Samaritan bound the wounds of the
> beaten man with *elaion*.[21]

Those who pray the Jesus Prayer believe that through the repetition of this prayer, we will develop an unconscious and unceasing conversation between us and God, and will find ourselves living into the reality of God's closeness. Or put another way, that it will bring into the soul a quiet burning awakening of the Divine Hongi.

That can be hard for those of us brought up to believe prayer is more task oriented than that. But this prayer is about union with God. It's a "come and live with me" kind of prayer that helps close the gap between heaven and us. In my own experience, growing a relationship with God this way tends to naturally lead into more prayer for others and the world anyway because He feels so much more interested and involved.

By regularly praying the Jesus Prayer, or something like it, we are awakening ourselves to what is already true whilst simultaneously inviting God to make it so: God is pouring His love out over us, we're living in it. It helps awaken our minds to this reality and trains us to live in the world through and in God, rather than beside or apart from Him.

If you're from a less traditional church background, like I am, regular and prescribed prayer can sound off-putting. But the intention with a prayer like this isn't to get stuck in our minds, it's to give them a lane to move in. And remember, it's not meant to be a mental exercise (though it may feel that way at first); the prayer is to be prayed with the mind in the heart. I've found that repetitive prayer like this, much like memorizing and meditating on Scripture, often gives my heart something tangible to hold on to before God whilst focusing my thoughts toward Him.

Christians were taught to practise the Jesus Prayer in focused times during their usual prayer times by repeating it over and over for a set period and then bringing it to mind whenever they could during the day. Personally, I practise just saying "Jesus" often when I'm at home in the chaos of my three young boys, during hectic workdays, and on family trips when I've no time to myself. The Jesus Prayer comes and goes from my life as it's helpful and needed.

I wasn't taught the Jesus Prayer. I discovered it in the years after my newfound experience of beholding as I sought to find context and language for this new way of life I was discovering. But the process of bringing the mind down into the heart, and speaking Jesus' name from that place, gives perfect expression to how I began to discover beholding, and it's invited me deeper as I've practised it since.

The Jesus Prayer, or saying Jesus' name like this, brings a deep sense of God's withness to me during my harder health seasons when I'm suffering migraines, fatigue, or brain fog. During those times it's often all I can muster, and I'm learning that for my Father in heaven, it's always enough.

All this sounds ancient and spiritual, but oddly enough, this practice was one of my greatest accidents as I was trying to figure out prayer in my early faith during my twenties, long before my season of learning to become a beholder. As I was awakening to the idea that God could be felt and known throughout my day-to-day life, I used to pray something far more simple and far less poetic. I endeavoured every moment I could to remember to say "Hey, God" out loud. When I was driving, whilst I was busy, or as I was waking or sleeping, I just started throwing out dozens of "Hey, Gods" into my day.

It had a profound effect on me. It slowly trained my mind and soul to expect God to be with me in some way all the time. I genuinely started to experience life in Divine Hongi. Everything just felt different. Not in some kind of perfect, euphoric way, but in a gradual, coming-into-God-awareness kind of way.

I noticed too that my behavior was changing. In the knowledge that God was with me, I felt more rested and still. My expectations changed as well, and it felt as though God could commune with me in every moment in my life, no matter how ordinary the circumstances.

Over my life I've moved in and out of this kind of existence. I'm definitely not suggesting that through praying this way I live in unbroken, perfect awareness of God in every moment (my kids help remind me of that!). But I can say from experience that praying this way moves us closer to the life we were created for— closeness with God in our ordinary and all-the-time lives.

I love the way another saint, a Russian starets from the nineteenth century, St Theophan the Recluse, described this way of existing:

> The essential part is to dwell in God, and this walking before God means that you live with the conviction ever before your consciousness that God is in you, as he is in everything: you live in

the firm assurance that he sees all that is within you, knowing you better than you know yourself. This awareness of the eyes of God looking in your inner being ... searching your soul and your heart, seeing all that is there ... is the most powerful lever in the mechanism of the inner spiritual life.[22]

Notice the flow for St Theophan: Firstly, we carry the conviction of Reality, that God lives within us. We practise faith. Secondly, that births the realisation that His living within us gives Him a profound access to our deepest parts, parts of us that even we ourselves struggle to access. He knows all our thoughts even before we think them.[23]

From there, St Theophan says, beholding flourishes. We come to the profound and beautiful awareness of this relationship of seeing. We don't often think of this kind of awareness and consciousness of God as prayer. Maybe because it seems less "do-ey" than other forms. But it's the bedrock. The way of living from which love comes to flow and every other form of prayer becomes alive.

God searching us within, seeing us with love and compassion, knowing us in this way and living our lives from the seat of this awareness. This is the idea of the Divine Hongi. This is the beholding life.

Living a life of beholding is about living life as it was intended, in Divine Hongi. The gospel is the story of this being invited into God. But to live that way, to awaken to it as our reality and not to the distance and distraction we so often feel, takes practice and an expanded way of approaching prayer. The idea of the Divine Hongi invites us to see prayer not as an intellectual exercise, or a transactional one, but an engulfment in God experienced by praying with the mind down in the heart.

It helps us to imagine prayer first and foremost as living in God-awareness.

The Jesus Prayer is an ancient way Christians have practised leaning into this God-soaked life. Like a marriage, which is true from its wedding day and is made more true as it's lived out between two people through the many seasons of their lives, the Jesus Prayer both awakens us to the reality that we are already inside God and invites Him to make it more true.

As I wrestled my way through moving from a transactional relationship to friendship with God, Divine Hongi became the way I was experiencing Him. I was, even if ever slowly, learning to still myself for a while and to allow my mind to sink down into my heart to pray. There, I was seeing God, not with my eyes, but with my being. I was learning to behold Him, and prayer was increasingly becoming an experience.

The more I practised being with God this way, the more prayer started to bleed out into my every-moment life. God was becoming uncontainable.

It's still, of course, an ongoing process for me. I'm no master, but doing life with God this way helped me to grasp what communion can be. To see my life tangled with God, as He's always longed for me to experience Him.

Chapter 5

THE ART OF OTHER SEEING

"When I first saw God, I went a kind of blind.
Now all I see is Heaven in the eyes of enemy
and friend alike."

Prayer Vol. 01

"When I close my eyes to the other,
I have closed my eyes to You."

Prayer Vol. 02

"'Love the Lord your God with all your heart
and with all your soul and with all your mind.'
This is the first and greatest commandment.
And the second is like it: 'Love your neighbor as yourself.'
All the Law and the Prophets hang on
these two commandments."[24]

Jesus Christ

The wonder and mystery of God has been written into the DNA of every person on earth. Each one of us is a cosmos in and of ourselves and each more complex than first appearances might offer. When we look at another person, we're looking at a unique piece of the mind of God. A manifestation of His love that will, in history at least, only last the lifetime of that person before it vanishes again from the earth.

Like a sunset, God never duplicates us. He weaves a unique revelation of Himself into every person so that, in the words of Ephesians 2:10, we are each a masterpiece with our own quality, contour, and story. A mosaic both on display to the world and yet full of hidden wonder that only God gets the grand view of. We see the outer shells of these masterpieces in others, but it takes the eyes of the Spirit and a willing heart to see the wonder within.

When we look at humanity through the artist eyes of God, we see little miracles in everyone we meet—even our enemies. The church becomes a kind of artistic, anthropological priesthood, documenting and celebrating every little detail of our differences. As an opportunity to find God, being hospitable to another person, to any other person at all, becomes an act of Christ-embrace (as we'll soon see).

Something powerful and surprising happened to me as I learned to sit with God differently. When I was living in a transactional faith, subconsciously earning God's approval by working hard in ministry and yet aching to receive His accepting love, I tended to judge others in the same way. It makes sense really: we can't treat people more lovingly than God treats us, and if He's most interested in our sin, then that's how we're likely to relate to others too.

But as I changed to receiving God's love and practising not trying to earn it, I slowly learned to love and see others with an openness I'd never experienced. Other-love didn't feel as forced anymore; it felt natural, right even. Not that it was easy, but it was at least starting to make the most sense. By learning to behold and be beheld by God, I was gradually doing the same with others.

SEEING THOSE WE DON'T UNDERSTAND

Beholding others is about approaching people as we do God, as a mystery to discover and enjoy rather than to sense-make and control. Our beholding God moves the emphasis of our most essential relationship, our relationship with Divine Love, from being *understanding* oriented to *being* oriented, and as we practise being with God in this way, we're opening up room within ourselves to see those imaged after Him similarly. To learn to live in hongi with them as well. Because the way we relate to God is the prototype for the way we relate to everyone else.

Imagine if we had to understand God to be with Him; we would never reach a deep enough knowledge to make us feel like we could be close. In theological language we call this "faith seeking understanding." We believe first and then seek to make sense and learn the shape of Him whom we believe in.

In the process we can still be close to Him because what we *do* know about Him is the most important stuff: that He is good, kind, vulnerable, and willing toward us and that He will never act with evil toward us.

Knowing this fundamental goodness about God means we can be with Him whilst we grow in our understanding of the rest. God's goodness is what our relationship is based on. Beholding others is simply our treating others with that same dignity.

If our gospel is sin obsessed, it reduces our story with God to that of forgiveness only, and we're likely to take that sin-central view of life to those around us. Sin will be the first thing we see, and when we're confronted with people who touch the nerve of our particular sin horror, we will struggle to see their image. We'll only see their brokenness as the main event of their existence.

If our gospel is one of reconciliation, if it begins before the fall in Genesis with God's face-to-faceness with us, then we're more likely to see that essential good in someone first and prioritize their rediscovering friendship with their Father over moral correction. We'll see their image, their imago Dei.

In a strange and smaller way, I know exactly how this feels. The more I've shared my story of chronic illness over the years in the hope of encouraging others going through similar journeys, the more it has made its way into how people see me. And that makes total sense. It's a big part of my life, my ongoing story of who I am.

Imagine if we had to understand God to be
with Him; we would never reach a deep enough
knowledge to make us feel like we could be close.

My illness can also become all people see of me, though, categorising me in a particular way. I can find myself quickly fielding questions or having conversations about it and, often, get drawn toward a natural remedy someone has found to work or the latest article that claims to create breakthroughs in chronic illnesses like mine. I don't fault people for that at all; it's human nature, and in many cases it's because people really care. I'm so grateful for that.

But I'm also so much more than whatever my body is going through, and I don't want my relationships to be built around the broken aspects of my life. I have a thriving inner life, a beautiful family; I love following international politics, reading great books, and hunting down the best single-origin coffee in town. It takes consideration and forethought for people to go there with me first. It takes beholding me as more than my limitations.

Now, if that's how I feel about others' compassionate and caring approach to my ongoing health, I can't imagine how those whose brokenness is more socially side-eyed, grave, or harder to understand must feel. I can also see why it was so powerful when Jesus saw past all the obvious sin in people's lives to love the whole person instead, and why the hypocritical leaders of His day were so confounded.

The woman at the well in Samaria in John 4 is a beautiful example of this. Jesus was confronted with a woman who had had many husbands and was not married to the man she was presently with. One divorce alone would have had a powerful negative connotation for this woman, and being in her current relationship would have socially marked her further. It would have been all that many would have seen first when they spoke to her.

But not Jesus. Jesus beheld her. He asked her for water, drawing her into a deeply spiritual conversation, one that He didn't dive into with the all-together religious leaders back in Jerusalem. Jesus saw something else; He saw deeper than this woman's mistakes. He saw someone longing for God with the capacity to be a great evangelist. When her relationships did come up, Jesus didn't lecture her on sexual ethics; He continued to invite her into the story of God.

And she did become an evangelist. So much so that Jesus stayed for days in the town where she lived as she drew many others out to hear Him.

Jesus did this kind of thing all the time. He saw the beauty in others louder than their shortfalls. It's so unnatural for us to do this if we're sin obsessed. To transcend others' shortfalls and love like Jesus, we need to become beholders.

It's not an either-or, of course, because one can't be fully reconciled without a transformation of the behaviors that bring relational brokenness. But repentance was often a response to Jesus' profound love and grace toward someone, not the result of His direct confrontation or lecture on their brokenness. It matters that we choose to see someone's God-image before their sin. People are more than their brokenness.

When we see others through their God-image first, over and above what we can make sense of in the interim, we can love and behold them, because no matter how they act—enraging us, confusing us, or challenging us—we know that as surely as God is good, His good image is placed within that person and we can find common ground. This means that though we may not see eye to eye, we can allow the God in us to connect with the God in them in a dignifying way.

Practically, this means when we're talking with those we disagree with, no matter how our arguments end, we never denigrate the dignity or fundamental goodness of one another. Even our enemies. Even our political opponents. It means that when we see another at our borders, challenging our cultural norms, holding vastly different political views, asking more of our financial social situations than we think we can give, we're seeing God and the opportunity to meet and care for Him.

Even if that person seems to us to be the antithesis of who God is (through our understanding), we cannot deny their God-given human dignity (being). We can still behold them.

Beholding others is the practice of giving other people the same opportunity to be loved before being understood that we give

God. It means we prioritize being with and seeing others before categorising and confronting them. It gives us space to journey with others as they work through their own brokenness without making it a prerequisite for acceptance. It demotes answers and promotes togetherness. Sounds a lot like Jesus' ministry with His disciples to me.

Again, that's not to say that we're not seeking transformation or that sin doesn't matter. Love will always long for healing wherever it sees brokenness, and full reconciliation isn't possible without the healing of the brokenness within us. Beholding others doesn't mean resigning to their shortcomings or becoming indifferent, but it does mean that on the long journey toward healing and reconciliation, we can sit with each other and see each other with beauty and love.

BECOMING GODLY LISTENERS

As I was discovering, we can learn this art of beholding others in the tension of their lives by being with God in that same answerless tension ourselves. By learning to see Him not as a divine search engine but as a Person who longs to be with us. By learning to become good listeners.

If we walk with God for long enough, we'll experience seasons of dryness and quiet. Times when all our prayer, tears, longing, and searching will feel like they're turning up nothing. These seasons deeply challenge our assumptions that we can always feel, sense, or hear God when He's there, and we're forced to walk the faith journey in what feels like complete blindness.

It's often in these seasons that beholding prayer becomes a lifeline for our spiritual walk. Here, we're coerced to either behold God for who He says He is or deny Him altogether as we find we don't have the energy, faith, or mind space to wrestle with the questions anymore. Beholding prayer becomes a way of acknowledging that somehow God is sitting with us in the dust of it, strangely available, closer than our skin.

The Psalms come alive like living companions because like the psalmist's, our prayer finally becomes honest and raw. These hard times are a gift to us in this way, though they rarely feel like it in the moment. Through them we learn the silent companionship of God in our suffering. The quiet persistence of His love in the wilderness.

Over time we learn to look back and see that He was with us in awareness and acceptance even when we couldn't feel or see it in the moment. He wasn't withholding His love or presence from us by not giving us the answers or healing we wanted; He was demonstrating the audacity of His love to sit with us in our pain without giving them. He was just there with us in our grief much like He was whilst walking with Mary on the way to Lazarus' tomb. In our darkest moments, we were being beheld by God.

This may only make sense to someone who has experienced it themselves because it's not rational. Why wouldn't God give us the answers He knows we so desperately want? It's not like He could be out of ideas, right? You may know what it's like to sit with someone deep in grief, feeling like you may have a valuable answer or something to say, but knowing the person likely couldn't hear it. They couldn't hear it because it's not what they need.

When someone is at the height of grief, of almost any kind, what they really need is someone to share that cry with them, to sit in the questions, and to just be there. What they need is our silence, our empathy, our presence. Not necessarily our sense-making.

So it is with God and us. In our times of great trouble, this is what God is doing. He's beholding us. He proves His love of us by allowing Himself to be misunderstood whilst we respond with anger, accusations, and ache. That is the self-security of God. It's risky for Him because He knows how desperately we want quick and effective change, but He also knows there's more to love and knowing than that too. He is strong enough to love us and behold us even when we're vitriolic and wounded.

Throughout these seasons, if we can hold on with an open heart and humble acceptance, we'll learn the art of doing this for others. Being able to sit with someone in their grief and love them without changing them is a divine gift that needs to be experienced first with God. It's not natural for most of us. Pride wants to step in and fix things or come up with an easy answer.

As followers of Christ, we often want to make sense of the pain and suffering those around us are experiencing, to explain it away with our best theology or pat-on-the-back advice (I know I do), instead of letting all the mess just sit there between us. For the one who has beheld and been beheld by God through their own dark nights, allowing people to vent their honest anger and rail away at others and God is an act of genuine strength and compassion. They're able to let others fully be, as God once let them be.

Our world desperately needs this kind of presence today. So much of the pain in people's lives is coming from a deep unheard-ness. Everyone is talking, few are listening. I like to imagine a world in which the church can become God's ears to the world. Listening with this kind of grace, sitting with others in their darkness, teaching them how to *be* in the tension of pain and the wonder of life.

Today, as a whole world of people feel despair and depression at historic levels, maybe God longs to fashion a priesthood of believers who know how to sit in the darkness alongside them with enduring love, even when it feels helpless. We've been really good at talking, sometimes talking at people, for a long time. What if it's time to learn to listen as a form of witness? What if deep listening is a way of healing the world, of revealing God to it?

In this way, we can be present as a form of mission for our times, helping others to make sense of their pain, suffering, loneliness, confusion, success, and blessings in the context of God's withness. As we behold and love in these ways, that love engulfs people into the kind of relationship with us that God longs to have with the world. It shows them a little more of what God is like.

We're the closest thing to God for many on this earth; we're Christ's body. So when we love the image of God in others and sit with them in a beholding manner, we give them a sample of the magnificent and all-engulfing love of God too. It makes engulfing love a witness; it makes the arms of compassion the reach of God to the lost.

Everyone is talking, few are listening. I like to imagine a world in which the church can become God's ears to the world.

In more recent times, it seems what's mattered most to our gospel sharing has been the transfer of beliefs: an emphasis on talking over listening. But Christ was a great listener, spending much of His time with the poor, sick, and ashamed that came to Him being present and available. Beholding sees listening to the world and sitting with them as just as important to their salvation journey as their understanding of theology; the godly presence of a good listener is theology embodied. Both together show the truth and nature of Christ.

Not all of us are called to the vocation of an evangelist, but the universal calling of every follower of Jesus is that of being witnesses to what we have seen and touched[25] and of those who have been seen and heard by God. Beholding invites us to be witnesses through our attentive and compassionate listening, as well as through our storytelling and sharing.

Reconciling love adores every person as they are because they see God even when they can't yet see Him themselves. They can see God because they slow down enough to put their own ideas aside and see the person who is, not the one who isn't.

It's important to note that this doesn't mean we should keep our mouths closed about important issues in the fear that we may offend people or that it may cause them to feel less seen. That's another extreme, and it's not even the best way to love someone. But love changes our volume, our temperament, the words we use, and the place we challenge from.

Reconciling love changes our tone. It makes us, hopefully, slower to speak and more willing to offer the benefit of the doubt to those on the other side of the table from us. It refuses us the opportunity to speak harshly and invites us to speak from beside rather than across from others. It becomes harder to lob verbal grenades at our enemies or those we hate when we see so much God in them. Imagine an age of politics that looked and sounded more like this.

One practice I've made in the past is to imagine my enemies sitting on God's lap as His children, prodigal or otherwise, when I talk or think about them. It changes the very language I use and the future I hope for them. In truth, this is always the reality. Every person is a child of God in the sense that He has made them. Every person is either one of the ninety-nine or the one that is lost, but both are His sheep. God is equally passionate about both.

Listening to others like this is a form of hospitality. It makes room for their voices. This hospitality is offered and extended every time we cry with the mourner, sit with the lonely, forgive our enemies, walk further with those who demand it from us, refuse division based on fringe ideologies, keep our word, and stand against injustice.

I don't believe any of this is possible without God. True other-love is a miracle, and I think our polarized world today demonstrates that. My emerging transformation in how I saw and experienced others was a wonderful accident, an unexpected fruit of this new way of knowing God.

In truth, as much as it was helping me to see God in those I hadn't before, especially in the marginalised, it also made me more passionately opposed to hypocrisy and those who oppress others. But it wasn't with an unhealthy anger or self-righteousness, at least not most of the time; it was more out of a desire to protect the God I saw in others.

Beholding prayer changes how we experience God knowing us, and in turn, it gives us a whole new way of relating to and loving others. A way that reshapes traditional ways of seeing evangelism, making us hospitable people, sharing God's nature with His truth and embodying the Kingdom we're communicating in our jobs, vocations, and families.

It helps us to put sin back where it belongs, behind God's image in every other. Not so we can minimize the damage and destruction that sin does to people and the world, but so we can begin where God begins, with a child deeply loved, needing to be brought home. It also changes the nature of our conversation within the church, lowering the temperature, demanding we hold one another in dignity even when the disagreement is over things that deeply matter to us.

In a lonely and loud world where people are commodified and used for gain by industries and individuals alike, our simply sitting with and hearing others can be a powerful witness, revealing what God is really like to the world.

Chapter 6

THE IMPORTANCE OF EATING GOD

"I'm learning to discover You,
in the minute and ordinary, God.
Your kingdom is as miniature as it is vast."

Prayer Vol. 02

"When I stop, and wait,
I discover You over in
some unnoticed place,
doing what I hadn't asked,
being God despite me."

Prayer Vol. 03

"Very truly I tell you,
unless you eat the flesh of the Son of Man and drink his blood,
you have no life in you."[26]

Jesus Christ

A danger in using language like *beholding, prayer,* and *spiritual experience* is that we might struggle to plant it all in our daily lives. We hear a lot of talk of spirituality today, from quasi health spiritualists to a wider embrace of Eastern spiritual views and a growing fascination with magic, death, alien life, and the paranormal. Yet the auto-blender of consumerism continues to slosh it all together in a cultural soup of unhinged capitalism, inequality, anger, division, and hyper-individualism, driving us further into our own lonely burrows. All this spirituality, in other words, doesn't seem to be transforming us meaningfully and for the better.

If beholding is to have the kind of transformative power I'm suggesting, we're going to have to do better. We'll need to anchor it to our lives so that it doesn't, as skeptics of contemplative spirituality claim, fall victim to eternal navel gazing or become another self-improvement fad.

It will need teeth, and the kind of teeth that will happily sink into our families, workplaces, study, house cleaning, account keeping, and all the myriad of relationships that make up our social fabric. It's going to need to bridge the divide we often feel between our expectations of the God-life and its reality. To pull God much closer into us. To make Christ all.

One of my earliest memories of heart-aching prayer was during my first year of intermediate school as a twelve-year-old boy. During my lunch hour one day, I must have been particularly gripped by the desire to hear God's voice because I was walking the school grounds and weeping, asking to live a life of conversing with Him. I was always fascinated with the prophets and their ability to speak with God. If God existed, I thought, it had to be that or nothing.

For years I kept praying the same prayer, asking and yearning for God to speak to me. I was hoping for something definitive, something other-bodily, like a voice from heaven or an undeniable, open-eyed vision. But what came in time wasn't near-solid, movie-like images before me but faint impressions that required as much faith as any other part of my life with God.

If I hadn't been so obsessed with talking with God, I probably never would have investigated these impressions further, but I had made it my life's goal. So for years I prayed through, shared, and acted on them to see if they were Him. They were, and I learned through the whole process that God can sometimes feel subtle, ordinary, or familiar. Because God doesn't send emails; He speaks from within. He's earthy like that.

And that doesn't just apply to hearing His voice but also to experiencing His presence or noticing where He is and isn't moving. Often, our expectations of what God might look and feel like are so huge that if He were to move in our lives, we would miss the very subtle and natural ways He already is moving.

Of course, when I became unwell, I found this even more crucial because life felt mundane in the extreme. During those years as I sat around helplessly, God drew my attention to a way of living and understanding His presence that I'd never seen before. About what it means to live life engulfed in Him. And I saw the Divine Hongi in a surprising place: the mystery of the Eucharist.

REAL PRESENCE

The Eucharist is the name we give to the sacrament of the Lord's Supper. On the night before Jesus was crucified, He broke bread and poured wine, saying it was His body and blood. He told His disciples that whenever they gathered like they did that night, they should do the same in remembrance of Him. Since the earliest moments of the church, believers have done this together every Sunday, teaching that it is one of the unique ways that God meets, loves, and empowers His church with His grace.

This genuinely humble sacrament of eating bread and drinking wine (or juice) helps us to see, feel, and touch, literally, what life looks like when God fills it. It's the place where imaginary spirituality becomes earthed spirituality, and through some of the most widely shared and commonly held elements humanity has at her disposal.

Of all the ways Jesus might have commanded us to celebrate the mystery of His God-humanness, of what it looked like when God walked the earth as one of us, He chose this. It challenges our notion of what God does and does not touch and what He does or does not fill.

In the incarnation of Jesus, we experience God as someone who is unafraid of not only human flesh but human nature as well. We discover that the world and all its mundane responsibilities and necessities are no barrier for the miracle of divine life. In Jesus we ourselves are invited to be unafraid to be human and, even more shockingly, to see it as the home of God. In the Eucharist, as we'll soon see, we eat and drink of that very same reality.

As I was awakening to what it meant to bring all my humanity to God, I felt drawn to understand the Eucharist and what it had to teach me even more. So hang with me for a minute because I'd like to share a little church history and theology before talking about why it matters so much.

The early church, and the majority of the church ever since, has held that every time the church gathers to celebrate the Eucharist together, in some mystical and yet actual way, when we consume that bread and wine, we're also consuming Jesus. This isn't necessarily the same as transubstantiation, which seeks to explain the exact mechanics of how that might work. It's also not the symbolic view that some churches hold either. There are theologians who have gone to great lengths to either totally explain or keep mysterious exactly what is happening during the Eucharist. I'm not one of those and this isn't the place for it. But what I do want to offer is that there's a spacious way to hold the mystery of it, explained with the name Real Presence: that Christ is mysteriously yet substantially present in the Eucharist in a real and true way. In other words, when we drink the wine and eat the bread of the Lord's Supper, we are in some real way eating and drinking Christ's body and blood.

It may sound strange if you've never heard that before, but it has magnificent implications for our world, our bodies, and our communion with God. So if you can stay with me, allow me to share how, even if you don't abide by Real Presence yourself, it can still offer tremendous beauty to your communion with God.

Recently my eldest son asked me about the mechanics of the Trinity, and I told him, "Jesus is both 100 per cent man and 100 per cent God." My eldest is nine years old and a keen mathematician, and he was quick to point out that my statement was, in fact, impossible. He must be 50/50 instead. "I know, right?" I replied. "That's the mystery of it. It's hard, even impossible, for us to grasp, and that's what it's like to know God sometimes." It's possible for Jesus to be all man and all God, and though it can seriously challenge our notion of things, it's the centre of the story of salvation.

Real Presence makes sense like that, as a mystery we can be sure of.

But where does this understanding come from? This view of the Eucharist as Real Presence is consistent from Scripture to the early church fathers and mothers. First, in a prophetic declaration that would only later make sense to many of His disciples, Jesus declared, "Very truly I tell you, unless you eat the flesh of the Son of Man and drink his blood, you have no life in you. Whoever eats my flesh and drinks my blood has eternal life, and I will raise them up at the last day."[27]

Later, St Paul wrote to the Corinthians to remember, "Is not the cup of thanksgiving for which we give thanks a participation in the blood of Christ? And is not the bread that we break a participation in the body of Christ?"[28]

But did the early church interpret those messages so literally? The writings of the early church fathers certainly seem to say so. St Justin Martyr in his *First Apology* (AD 151) said:

> For not as common bread nor common drink do we receive these; but since Jesus Christ our Savior was made incarnate by the word of God and had both flesh and blood for our salvation, so too, as we have been taught, the food which has been made into the Eucharist by the Eucharistic prayer set down by Him, and by the change of which our blood and flesh is nurtured, is both the flesh and the blood of that incarnated Jesus.[29]

Notice that Justin Martyr's argument for how Eucharist can be Jesus' actual body and blood is based on the mystery of the incarnation. His claim is that it's possible and true because Jesus' God-humanness is. The Eucharist is the sacrament that embodies that reality.

Shortly after, Irenaeus taught the same, "If the Lord were from other than the Father, how could He rightly take bread, which is of the same creation as our own, and confess it to be His body and affirm that the mixture in the cup is His blood?"[30] (AD 189), again basing his understanding of the Eucharist on the mystery that Jesus Himself was human *and* divine also and therefore changes how we understand other physical things being transformed miraculously too. Later Augustine in his *Sermons* (AD

411) explained, "What you see is the bread and the chalice; that is what your own eyes report to you. But what your faith obliges you to accept is that the bread is the body of Christ and the chalice is the blood of Christ,"[31] inviting us to continue this tradition of receiving it in faith, not sight.

But how is that possible? Are we really meant to believe that the Eucharist is Christ's actual body and blood when it looks, tastes, smells, and feels exactly as the bread and wine did before it was blessed? This very question is why the Eucharist is called a sacrament. The word *sacrament* itself being derived from the Greek *mustérion*, which is where we get our word *mystery*, and as we've already seen, a great mystery it is.

The bread and wine look the same, taste the same, and smell the same, but in the Eucharist they've become enchanted by the Spirit. They've mysteriously become Christ to us.

It's a mystery in the same sense that full spiritual regeneration occurs in us during baptism, and we are born again in God. Externally we look exactly how we used to, though with a little more life in the eyes. But in reality we are a "new creation."[32] And as already mentioned, it's also in the same manner that somehow Jesus could be totally God and totally man simultaneously without tension, issue, or compromise.

It's a miracle that demands to be embraced, not sense-made, to fully appreciate its beauty. Or as my friend and mentor Bishop Bruce Gilberd put it, "In the Eucharist reality and mystery are fused; there is no either-or."

Wasn't it the same with Jesus? The living God Himself lived among humanity for decades unknown as such by those around

Him. Think about that: God lived, spoke, made tables, and laughed and cried amidst humanity in such an ordinary way that He lived undetected for most of His life. Even when He did "go public," He was still so much made up of normal stuff that He wasn't believed! In His form, Jesus looked sublimely ordinary. In His nature, He was shockingly divine.

And so it may also be with Eucharist.

Receiving Eucharist as the actual body and blood of Jesus doesn't require some kind of scientific, Enlightenment-era explanation. It requires us to approach the mystery of God with innocent faith. When we do, it has the power to transform the world. That's why this is so important. Because Jesus lived, died, resurrected, and ascended two thousand years ago. We could be forgiven for forgetting how ordinary and natural He must have seemed to the world around Him; we weren't there! But the Eucharist lives this truth out again and again in our present lives. It's an object lesson in what it must have been like to see Jesus, and an object lesson for what it looks like for God to fill you and me, right now, in our very ordinary worlds.

Two thousand years later God is still doing miraculous things with the ordinary stuff of our world. Including us.

WALKING WITH GOD IS MORE
NATURAL THAN YOU KNOW

Over the years I've often found myself in conversations with people who say, "I don't hear God, He doesn't speak to me," when I'm sharing my own story or someone else's story about a time God was leading. Whenever I hear it, I consider it my personal invitation to help them recognise how often God is speaking to them without their knowing it. It's a great feeling seeing them light up when they realise they've been hearing God all along, and I've never met someone who hasn't.

One night over dinner a friend told me God never spoke to her, so I asked her when she felt the most love or compassion. She told me that often, for no reason at all, she'll be walking the aisles of the supermarket and will see someone elderly or in need and just start weeping with love. "I have no idea why!" she said. "It's so random and embarrassing, but I just want to go over and hug them and tell them they're loved!"

I could see in her face before she even finished saying the sentence out loud her realisation that it had been God "speaking" to her in some powerful way. "I've never had that feeling," I told her. "I'm not sure that's a normal reaction to an elderly lady in the fruit section!" God was speaking to her through compassion and probably inviting her to share His love with someone else. But because it didn't sound like an audible voice, or come distinctly from how she experienced the rest of her life, she assumed it was random.

But God isn't random; He speaks Eucharistically.

I've had similar conversations with countless people who feel they don't hear God, and it causes real loneliness or a sense of disqualification for them. When someone stands up at church and says, "God told me …," we imagine that to say something with such certainty means they've been let in on the secret of getting God to speak to them in obvious ways. But more often than not, it's this Eucharistic voice they're expressing.

God "tells" them through deep senses within, a gentle and persistent "knowing," or a dream that strikes unusually in their mind until they contemplate it. All of it looks and sounds so ordinary until the moment you say, "Aha! I know now that it was God speaking to me." Next thing you know, you're sharing a story, skipping all those details, and simply saying, "God told me ..." God speaks through our emotions, intellect, daydreams, imaginations, and unspoken longings because God is Eucharistic. He fills the bread of our everyday inner communications.

Of course, all of that can be confused by what the church fathers called the "three enemies of the soul": the flesh, the world, and the devil. So it takes Scripture, community, and discernment— things that grow over time in our long journey of faith—to tell the difference. But what's important is that often the sound of the Spirit arrives to us far more ordinarily than we expect.

So many of us live our lives assuming that God is so different from our experience that if He spoke, or if He were to live in us as He promises, it would somehow feel totally *other*. We separate the "spiritual" from the mundane and ordinary because we don't appreciate how imaged after God we already are, and how natural it is for us to experience and know Him.

God speaks through our emotions, intellect,
daydreams, imaginations, and unspoken longings
because God is Eucharistic. He fills the bread
of our everyday inner communications.

This is staggering to me because whilst we often spend so much of our lives seeking the spiritually extraordinary, God came to us embodied in our mundane ordinary and said, "Look! This is what divine life looks like! To live fully alive, in obedience to, and in pleasure with Me is to be more human, not less!" And every time we take Eucharist together, we get an object lesson in this very truth. Because not only is a special and tangible grace poured out over us when we take it together, but we're also being reminded what a prayerful, God-soaked, and divine life really looks like.

This not only applies to hearing God's voice, but to our entire lives. So often we're participating in God's activities without knowing it. Because as it turns out, just as with Jesus, God's divine purposes are ordinary too. For thirty quiet years Jesus went about eating, cleaning, building, being a friend, being a son, being a participant in community. He lived this way because these are all good things God has made. And so is every aspect of our lives today.

When Katie and I found out we were having our first boy, we spent whole nights together talking and imagining what he'd be like. We knew he would look something a little like the both of us and so would his personality, but we couldn't really picture what that meant. How do you create an image of a living person out of nothing in your mind, even with all the things you know about yourselves as parents?

It was both exciting and frustrating for it to be so elusive. Then, when he was born, he was both nothing and everything like what we'd imagined. We knew the stuff that was going to make up his person—his DNA would be ours, his personality would reflect ours in some way, he would have certain coloured hair, skin, and size—but even with all that, we still couldn't predict the wonder of his person. For that, we needed him to be embodied, to be born.

That's what the Eucharist does for us. It lands our experience of God in our lives. We may know the theory of all the stuff that makes up a spiritual life, an encounter with God, or God's nature itself. But until we land it in an experience, we have no real map for knowing what it's supposed to look and feel like. Coming to the Eucharist with the faith that it's Christ's body and blood challenges our senses. Then we're invited to see the rest of our lives in the same Spirit-enlivened way.

This is why the incarnation of Christ—God becoming human—is so magnificent. "No one has ever seen God," wrote St John. "But the unique One, who is himself God, is near to the Father's heart. He has revealed God to us."[33] That "unique One" is Jesus Christ, and it's because of Him we don't have to be lost when we think about the metaphysics or mystical reality of experiencing God. If humans experienced Jesus and passed Him off as just an ordinary person, we're likely to make the same mistake in our own lives.

If it wasn't for Jesus, we might *imagine* what God could be like, and we might take the commandments and the Old Testament and have a crack at embodying them our way, but in Jesus Christ we get an exact picture. And goodness what a picture! Because of Jesus we know how the commandment "Love your neighbor as yourself" looks in practice. The Eucharist reminds us that the miracle of ordinary wonder didn't end with Jesus' ascension.

HEAVEN INVADES THE WORLD

The Eucharist invites us to accept how ordinary divine life can be, and when it comes to beholding, this is liberating. Sometimes when we pray and look out to God, all we see is nature, ourselves, quiet, or the day-to-day feelings of malaise and struggle we feel—the bread and wine. But with a Eucharistic mind, we can see too that those things aren't separated from God, but the places, people, and things His divine life is filling. We can see Him there.

To look at the world is to see Christ hidden amidst it, and though it may not always feel ecstatic or outer body, it's as valid as sharing a meal with Jesus in Cana, where before He transferred water into wine, He was just another ordinary guest. The Eucharist demands that we see the world enchanted.

The miracle of God filling ordinary stuff is that ordinary stuff suddenly becomes sacred and otherworldly again. The world becomes illuminated with God like it was in the Garden, a place for communing and meaning-making with Him. To say that God fills our mundane lives is the same as saying once we see the world Eucharistically, there is no such thing as the mundane. God is everywhere, and we're invited to transform every ordinary thing into holy things by loving God with and through them.

For thirty quiet years Jesus went about eating, cleaning, building, being a friend, being a son, being a participant in community. These are all good things God has made. And so is every aspect of our lives today.

Even a life lived fatigued and alone. Even a life that doesn't seem grand to the world. Like mine does during so many of my health-limited days.

We also have moments when we peek through and experience something heavenly—a vision, a dream, a physical healing, or a miracle of some kind. It would be an overreaction, and a travesty really, to expect God to only come to us as "life as usual." God has in the past and still does many very unusual things in my life. Think again about Jesus' life. God, embodied in human form, still did incredible things; He raised the dead, healed the blind, set oppressed women free from the tyranny of social structures, healed lepers, and preached with divine authority. All before giving us His Spirit to do the same.

But He also had downtime, slept at night like the rest of us, and had to clean and take care of Himself. Not to mention the thirty years of no miracles at all that we know of. The invitation is for God to fill this world every moment with Him, not for us to escape it, and that means a lot when it comes to divine communion.

This isn't "cooling" in the faith; it's maturing. It's the success of a beholding life, a Eucharistic life, that is pulling God into ourselves and the world. The invitation for us to re-see life, not to keep expecting life to become something else altogether. Does God still speak in dreams, visions, and giftedness in a Eucharistic world?

Absolutely, but those things will feel more and more natural, not less and less, and what we mean by "natural" will be more and more holy. Christ makes us more human, makes us more earthed, not less.

My journey toward understanding all of this was far less theological than experiential. I didn't have a good theology of the incarnation or sacrament when I started taking Eucharist seriously. I was from a nondenominational background that tended not to know what to do with physical, ordinary stuff. It seemed counter-spiritual to me.

But through my years of illness, and of sitting quietly before the world outside the bedroom window of the Franciscan retreat centre where I spent my time, I saw God more clearly in nature, in the rhythm of my breathing, and in the food I ate with the other guests. My head was often too foggy, my mind too unreliable, to meet with God in Scripture, theology, or continuous mental dialogue. I needed an existence-level communion, and that came with an awareness, thankfulness, and appreciation of the life I was living, for the bread and wine of my everyday life.

As beholding prayer transformed my life, I wasn't pulled away into a more "spiritual realm." It was the opposite; heaven invaded my ordinary, and God saturated me. It was as if my bones, skin, eating and drinking, and my simply existing became prayer. Prayer became about being human and being human toward God. That's why for me, the best definition of prayer is my gazing into God, gazing into me, gazing into Him. Because that can be done with my life as much as my conscious thoughts, which is something we'll explore more when we consider how our body prays in a beholding way.

This is why I chose the moniker Commoners Communion for my work in prayer. I had discovered that my relationship with God wasn't so much about praying as I'd understood it until then—how much I prayed or the kinds of prayer I was engaging in—but a union, an integration with God in my whole life that was so much greater than all of that. It was about Eucharistic living, about communion. And not for the hyper-spiritual, but for every human being.

My hope by sharing about Real Presence isn't to attempt to convince you of its Eucharistic theology. It's to invite you to see the world differently, to learn from the past, and to be inspired to grasp just how powerful what Jesus achieved in His incarnation really is for us.

Through a Eucharistic view of prayer God breaks in and heals our lives, making them holy. It transforms the way we approach prayer times *and* family and work time. It fills it with heaven. But I was also coming to see that the Eucharist isn't just about a single sacramental event, nor is it only about the vertical relationship between God and me. I was learning that it's also prototypical for my life in the world. An invitation to live a life of Eucharistic hospitality.

Chapter 7

SHARING THE TABLE

*"The unwelcome have become the welcomers
in the house of their God."*
Prayer Vol. 02

*"Blessed is the one who will eat at the
feast in the kingdom of God."*[34]

If God gave us a table as the central way for understanding and celebrating His life *in* us, then it stands to reason that it has something powerful to offer the world *through* us too.

Christian hospitality has been a hallmark of our outward love to the world since the birth of the church, leading to the founding of what is the hospitality industry today. That's because the early church understood the power of the table as a place for seeing and sharing God. A place, too, for beholding others and the world.

Because if Jesus was bread and wine to be eaten and drunk by any who were hungry and thirsty, then few other experiences could speak that reality with powerful simplicity to a lonely and divided world better than the dinner table. At the shared table, life is enabled and laughter, joy, grief, and acknowledgement find air. When we sit at any table, relationships can be healed or severed, life can be celebrated or mourned.

Eucharistic hospitality recognises the basic need every human has. The need to eat in order to live. Whether you're the most powerful person in the world or what some may consider the least significant, you need to eat and drink or you will die. We might pretend that some are more important than others, but the table proves otherwise. Wherever you sit or however you're dressed, you can't avoid this plain reality. The table is a sign of our weakness, limitedness, and mortality. It is a class leveler.

In the earliest years of the church, the table was revolutionary for this exact purpose. Roman rulers were desperate to stamp out this new Jewish sect called Christianity growing in their midst because it challenged their assertion that their emperor was god, not to mention their racist, sexist, and classist views of humanity. One of the ways the early Christians subverted this madness was by eating together. Men and women, Jew and Gentile, slave and free, Roman or otherwise, tax collector or priest, all sat at the table equally, radically disturbing the social and cultural prejudice of the day.

This was no accident; they'd already been taught that the Eucharist was for anyone who put their faith in Christ, regardless of their social demarcations. The early church was living a Eucharistic hospitality, and in first-century Israel, that beholding at the table helped change the social game.

Jesus calls the whole church to gather at the Eucharist, not parts of it or those who prefer to stick together. We may have different gifts and embark on different missional endeavours, one may favor hymns and the other more modern forms of song, your flatmates may be Pentecostal and your siblings Catholic, but in every circumstance Christ's commandment is the same: whenever you're together, "do this in remembrance of me."[35]

Here, the pastor and the congregant are equals, the adulterer and the liar, the Christian of fifty years and the Christian of fifty minutes, the local and the immigrant. We are all starved and in need of Christ's body which becomes the new standard for acceptance. Do you eat Christ? Then you belong. It's imperative we recognise that at the table of Christ, *He* is the centre. Not ultimately our church theology, practice, pastoral structure, or differences, as much as they do matter—but Christ.

At the Eucharist table, we all come exactly the same, as hungry children in need of what only God can give, Himself. There, our enemies, the outcasts, and the not-there-yets are all welcome to eat with us because the premise of our meal isn't perfection, wisdom, intellect, or self-discipline, it's Christ and the unifying truth that none of us belong there without His grace. As we behold Christ at Eucharist, we see His enemies as He does and as we were once: hungry people in desperate need of a crashing-in, transformative grace.

How can we stay enemies with someone we regularly eat with? How can we look down on another who shares Christ in the same special grace and power in the Eucharist as we do? If at the end of the day we're gathering to recognise our desperate need not just for earthly, physical sustenance but for the forgiveness and life-giving power of Christ, how could we possibly spend our days abusing or forgetting others who are not like us?

In worldly hospitality we may be afforded the opportunity to stick to our circles, but in Eucharist we're forced out of them and into Christ to share Him with the stranger. The oppressor, even. Beholding God through the Eucharist, then, has the power to transform how we see every other table too.

It's imperative we recognise that at the table of Christ, He is the centre. Not ultimately our church theology, practice, pastoral structure, or differences, as much as they do matter—but Christ.

At the table, we behold simultaneously Christ and every other, and not just in a symbolic way, but in a mysterious and rich way in which the Spirit moves on us to do something often unseen and unfelt. It saves us from our differences and spiritual short-term memory. It's radical, more radical than I think we've given it credit for in many of our churches.

What if we not only partook in the Eucharist this way when we met as Christian communities, but we saw it as the central paradigm for understanding our place in the world and with others too? So when we came to conversations or people that confronted us, we thought less in transactional spirituality—who is right, who is wrong, and how we agree—and more in a Eucharistic spirituality where we were all welcome to the table to sit under the lordship of Christ as we accepted our wrongness and rightness.

Maybe this vision of the Eucharist as our leading image could help us share meals with those we've persecuted for decades and even centuries, whether they're other religions, denominations, opposing political parties, or even church leaders who have let us down or hurt us. If it was enough for Jesus to share the table with His murderer the night before His death, then it must be enough for us to share a table with our enemies. The more we practise Eucharist, the more it transforms us and the way we eat.

Importantly, this doesn't mean a loss of truth or diversity or acknowledgement of brokenness and the very real issues we face in the world. We don't ignore or forget all that; we just place it where it belongs: before God. Remember, bread is broken in Eucharist, but often our conversations and relationships will be the same. The table isn't a place where the pain and grit of the world are left behind; on the contrary, they're engulfed and loved by God, given back as Christ. The joy of the wine and the brokenness of the bread are always there together. This means we can approach the real issues we face with others in the world as we would at dinner with guests: from a place of welcome, love, honesty, and humility.

The truth is, we all also bring our own brokenness, prejudice, and mess to the table, and if we're doing it well, we should be confronted by our own ignorance and inability to understand and share the world of others. Because the table isn't only about me, it's about the stranger, and even Christ was a stranger to me once. It wasn't until I was invited to His table, and came, that Christ became a friend. To draw near to God here is to draw near to every other He's inviting. That's confronting, because when that's what it becomes, and I see the kind of company I keep—the broken, the needy, the sinful, and the lost—I also see myself.

When we take Eucharist together and we look out to the world to engage in Eucharistic hospitality, we're giving up eating, drinking, and sharing for selfish reasons, and recentring our gathering on something and someone other. It challenges us to think differently about how we partake in our most basic needs. It challenges us to let go of self for the search and celebration of others and the world.

A few years ago, I was on the phone in the dairy aisle of the supermarket being verbally attacked. This person, someone close to me, was furious and they were accusing me of being the most selfish, deceitful, and dishonourable person they knew. They wouldn't let me speak, and their voice was so loud on the other end of the phone that people were looking at me as they walked by.

Nothing this person was saying was fair; it was all based on assumption and misunderstanding. I'm not perfect, I've made plenty of mistakes relationally in my life, but these accusations were not founded in any of them. I was furious and walked outside the supermarket to launch more privately into an offence before the Spirit not so gently confronted me and told me to humble myself and apologise. Because although this person's conclusions were wrong, God showed me that I hadn't loved and cared and been attentive enough to this person, and for that, I was in the wrong.

So I took the blows and apologised, genuinely apologised, that I'd allowed all this confusion and misunderstanding to come between us. I owned my part in not loving enough to quell the onslaught of bitterness my friend felt. I told them that I'd been very sick and struggling to stay afloat for the three or so years they were accusing me of not being present enough, but that wasn't an excuse to not reach out and keep in touch. I apologised for accidentally hiding that from them and not better explaining that we were struggling to get by, let alone keep up with what others needed from us. I didn't say it manipulatively; I was genuinely sorry that I hadn't been more open during that time.

What happened next was not at all what I was expecting. After almost twenty minutes of full-on abuse, they stopped, apologised in return for falsely accusing me, and shared the incredibly tough journey they had been on personally. They were suffering insomnia, depression, loneliness, and anxiety and admitted that all of that was pouring out on me unfairly as they tried to just make it through a single day without a panic attack. I asked if they could come to our place for dinner that week to share a meal with us and to reconnect, and I mentioned that we'd love to have them round every month for the rest of the year to stay in touch.

We did, and it was beautiful. We never spoke about the accusations; we didn't need to. Sharing a bottle of wine and some dinner in our own home, in our own presence for a few hours those nights, was enough to show them we weren't the people they'd assumed we were, but that we were well-intentioned yet imperfect people who had made mistakes without meaning to hurt them. Over the table, with a Eucharistic heart, our relationship was more than just healed, it was reconciled, and we began to grow closer and closer. Somehow, sitting together in that vulnerable and open place became the physical act that opened the spiritual door to friendship.

We didn't practise Eucharist those evenings, but they had a Eucharistic shape. By choosing to rebuild our relationship based on the presence of Love around the table, we were honouring Christ's call to eat our way into reconciliation with others and creation. By choosing to heal through those meals, we were sharing what Christ does with us every week through the sacrament, bringing us back around a meal to square things up and give us new graces. Eucharistic living is about taking what the table is to us and embodying it in our living out toward a world starved for love and acceptance. That's what makes it such a powerful beholding image.

As we've seen, the Eucharist is about fundamental sustenance. But another way of seeing it is as a place of profound simplicity. There is the Divine Mystery, yes, but there are also the most basic elements of life: food and drink. It isn't ultimately about complex theology, though this incredibly simple act is powerfully deep; it's about eternity breaking into our normal stuff. For me, this makes it a powerful place for reorienting our world around a simple spirituality when often we can make it seem far too complicated. It also offers us a more embodied one.

Jesus' disciples probably didn't really understand much of the weight of what was going on that first night Jesus led them through the Lord's Supper, but that wasn't the point. Because the table isn't mental assent but about receiving Christ and letting Him be enough. It is a physical act that invites us into a spiritual reality. So when we eat and drink together with the intention of celebrating Christ's life, death, resurrection, and return, we're embarking on the highest form of theology in the most practical and ordinary way. God distilled so much in the Eucharist that to spend our lives exploring this one incarnational act would be enough to keep us full for a lifetime. He also demonstrated the need for offering a simple and edible gospel to the world.

The table isn't only about me, it's about the stranger, and even Christ was a stranger to me once. It wasn't until I was invited to His table, and came, that Christ became a friend.

In His humility, God gave us a community-centring event that was accessible to every class, level of education, culture, and place using some of the most accessible material of our everyday lives. If we eat together, with Christ at the centre, we're living a robust, ordinary, and yet mystical spiritual faith in Jesus. This feels like a huge relief for me. This feels like the gospel for everyone. This feels to me like a place I can begin, and never finish beginning in. Because if it's the ordinary stuff of grain and grapes that God visits in communion to make it Christ, then it's the ordinary stuff of my day-to-day life that I can trust He'll do the same with. Eucharistic life is one where the mundane is made sacred and creation becomes the table of beholding in our minute-to-minute living.

I've often thought of prayer as sitting at the table with God at the end of the day over dinner. When I think of prayer in that way, it becomes communion: an opportunity to share space and catch up on each other's presence. A place of retreat and respite where my Father can ask me how I'm doing and I can share the good, the bad, and the aching. Prayer as a conversation, or as simply sitting in silence with God at the table, changes the very words we use and how we position our hearts for receiving. Eucharistic spirituality embeds God in my life and creates a home for us to live together. It makes the language of prayer, beholding, and God-experience something to be held and known, not just some far-flung language, and it helps me to embody that same hereness to the world.

Chapter 8

ON DEVOTION

"You've given me the work
of uncrowding,
of quieting a noisy soul,
preparing You the way,
that Beauty may sweep
promptly in, through the
passage of a heedful heart."

Prayer Vol. 03

"To hurry, is to vanquish
God's little gaps, designed
for divine opportunity."

Prayer Vol. 03

"But the worries of this life, the deceitfulness of wealth
and the desires for other things come in and choke the word,
making it unfruitful."[36]

Jesus Christ

A beholding people understand that as amazing as understanding and knowledge are, revelation—the process of information being transformed into knowledge through relationship to the Source— is the currency of Christ in a world of opposing opinions. And *that* requires a life dedicated to personal devotion.

Devotion is the attention we give to God. It's not emotion, though a devotional life leads to a sensitivity of feelings. It is the rhythms and moments of our days, weeks, months, and years that open communing space. Devotion isn't ritual, but it is ritualistic. It isn't working, but it is about works. It's about laying hold of our lives in such a way that they become containers for the Spirit of God to fill, creating a counter-liturgy to the gravitational draw of technology, entertainment, and the endless purchasing of things.

I've learned over the years that devotion isn't reliant on how spiritually powerful we feel we are. If we have seconds, minutes, and hours in our day, then we can devote our lives to a living affection for God. Because devotion is about making space, and we all have it in some shape or form.

When we wake in the morning, we can choose to devote time to God in the same way we devote our bodies to food, hygiene, and exercise. We don't call those things ritualistic or religious; we don't have breakfast with a sense of romanticism and heightened emotional experience. We do those things because we're alive and because they're good.

Becoming a people of prayer is saying that as worthy as our stomachs are of food, our bodies are of cleansing, our lungs are of breathing, God is even more of our attention. And it's about building habits throughout our day to live into it. If we leave eating to chance, we'll likely find ourselves oscillating between irritable hunger and satisfaction. Likewise with God, without planning in rhythm, we'll experience Him in boom and bust. Seasons of wonder and seasons of confusion and frustration.

That's not to say that creating a daily prayer habit will suddenly remove seasons of dryness and doubt, or make God felt as and when we want Him. He is God, and mystery, after all. But what our habits will do is, day by day, year on year, build a place for God to meet us in the times and ways He longs to, helping us to see a little clearer whether our dry seasons are self-inflicted or God driven. Our habits become altars of availability. God does the rest.

The truth is, it's not our job to fill our moments with God or with glory; it's His. It's our job to create the space for Him to do that Himself. That's why a devoted heart is somewhat ritualistic. We're ritualistic about the way we bring ourselves to God, and when we do, He fills it with relationship. A devoted life builds little altars for God to meet us.

When we want to get to know someone, we put in the effort to create the best spaces to do it. For romantic interests we organize dates and meaningful moments, for friendships opportunities to connect, eat, and do life together. All that organization doesn't make a good friendship or relationship, only people can do that. But having a good relationship without a little life-admin is impossible too. Relationships don't happen in a vacuum.

In my own experience, to really build a life of devotion, playing the long game is a far better strategy. I've slowly built little rhythms into my life over decades of trial and error, accepting what I can't do and leaning further into what I can. I've learned it's better to take one small practice—for example, five minutes of silence in the morning before a candle, prayer journaling, or reciting the Lord's Prayer during work breaks—and weave that into my life for three months before adding another.

It can feel exciting to map out a fervent new prayer life of hours a day, fasting, silence, intercession, or beholding time, but the reality is that in most cases we can't do it all at once. And if you're like me and have young kids and a household to keep running, there are often natural limitations to how much we can control our own rhythms.

The problem with unrealistic goals in prayer is that when we fail at doing it all, we might give up on doing anything. I'd rather do one small practice with commitment and definition than many poorly. God is in the quality, not quantity, business. I'm personally convicted that having a daily God-awareness through something like the Jesus Prayer, and seeking an inner stillness, has far more effect than intense morning devotions alone. Anyway, beholding is best done without all that angst and self-pressure. It's a relationship, remember.

Great books have been written on all the different forms of prayer that build a good life of communion. If you search "spiritual practices" or "spiritual disciplines," you'll find lots of good ideas. I'm not an expert on these practices, and for me, that's not how I came to build a life of prayer habits either. But I want to share with you a few things that have helped me create the kind of life I can live into without having to think about it every day.

A way to live in communion with God.

UNNOISING

Christ came to offer us a more beautiful life. A life immersed in joy and peace. We only have to look out at creation in all its colour, vastness, extremes, and complexity to see that God wants us to know the range of Him. There didn't need to be colour, sunsets, or coral reefs for life to exist. The Spirit could have made us totally functional without all that. But He didn't. He made a cosmos within and a cosmos without, to continually call to us all that life is meant to be fully lived, fully felt, and fully beheld.

But we're often asleep to it. Too caught up in the lesser things life offers either because we've forgotten the wonder of a beholding life or because we've just been too busy for too long to look up. We created calendars for ourselves in an attempt to tame time, but all we did was fill them right up, having time wrap us up in itself, demanding more than we can give.

But life with God doesn't work so well squeezed into our schedules or into our technology-saturated minds. If we're filling our heads with music, information, and activities all the time, we can form ourselves into living noise buckets, with all kinds of things echoing through the chambers of our souls.

Then, when we come to pray, we feel like we're hitting a brick wall at a hundred miles per hour and, spiritually speaking, we are.

Unnoising is about crafting a life in which prayer doesn't feel so much like an aberration as a natural flow in and out of everything we do. It's about allowing space in our calendars to be present to ourselves and what we're doing rather than filling them up to the brim for the idol of productivity. It's about listening to less, consuming less information, and clearing the space in our souls so we can better distil the voice of God.

It's about simplifying life and learning to live more still.

You can think of unnoising in two ways, as both a slowing down and a thinning out in our lives. Slowing is about the *quality* of the things we're doing in our lives, and we can do lots of practical things to slow down. To become aware of God again, we can walk and drive more slowly, allow five-minute breaks between meetings just to sit, notice how we're feeling and the world around us, or park a little farther from the shops and walk.

Slowing can be about reading the book rather than listening to its audio version. Reading a physical book slows you and seats you somewhere. You can't multitask when reading a physical book (and in truth, you can't with any real quality whilst listening to one either), and holding it changes the way your brain pays attention and receives the story you're reading.

You'll be able to think of your own slowing practices too. The point, though, is to stop yourself running through life at a sprint and to become more aware of everything you're doing. You would be amazed at how even driving the speed limit, and not a mile more, can bring more stillness to your soul. Let that car pull in front of you; don't rush to the next destination. Your soul will follow suit.

As we become more present to the lives we're living, so do our thoughts. So does God. These very tangible, practical things we do have a direct impact on the stress levels and panic in our minds. They pull us out of hyperdrive and into a more meditative state.

Thinning, on the other hand, is more about the *quantity* of things in our lives. It's about watching fewer shows, listening to fewer podcasts, consuming less news and social media, and filling our calendars with fewer things to do. It may be having fewer but deeper friendships, deciding to try to achieve less in a day, working fewer hours (if that's possible), and speaking fewer words.

It involves creating healthy phone habits, like a set time for checking social media in your day (or deleting it altogether!), putting your phone to bed for the night after dinner and not waking it up until after breakfast, and the deeply satisfying act of deleting all the apps you can live without. Phones are possibly our greatest adversary for the beholding life in our time. (I'd highly recommend the work of the Center for Humane Technology on tips for reining it in.)

Notice, thinning is about less, not nothing, and only you will know the right balance. I have moments in my weeks when I don't allow myself to listen to podcasts because I need a break, like whilst I'm doing the dishes after the kids have just gone to bed. I choose not to have music on in my car all the time and, when I'm in really healthy habits, only check the news once a day.

Another crucial thinning act is in the area of what we watch. Our eyes are the filmmakers of our souls, and our brains are a great archive. So what we watch often makes its way into our being. The best thing we can do, especially for better discerning God's voice, is to give up the violence, sex, murder, or just general non-life-giving content we find in so much of our entertainment these days. But even aside from that, limiting how much we watch even the good stuff helps our brains to focus and pay attention off-screen.

Thinning is about keeping our minds clearer of the voices of the world and others so we can attune them better to God. Almost all the examples I've given here aren't sinful. It's not about cutting out sinful noise, just noise in general, so we can be more present to ourselves, life, and in turn, God in our daily rhythms.

Consider spending a week or two to take stock of how much time you spend reading, watching, listening to, or engaging with things other than God. A good way to tell whether our consuming patterns are leading to a beholding life or a shallow one is the ratio of prayer to everything else.

For example, it's easier to study, even the Scriptures, than it is to pray. But study alone can't change us in God's economy, nor can action—personal or social transformation—without the spiritual transformation that takes place exclusively in communion with God. It's possible for even the simplest person to become the wisest through constant time in God's presence, but it's not possible for the wisest, most well-read person to enter the kingdom of God without prayer. In this way, our consumption habits reveal our true theology.

In God's economy, transformation happens through revelation, not knowledge acquisition. What I mean is that knowing more information about God, or about prayer even, won't transform us or draw us nearer to Him. The Pharisees and Sadducees who were near-perfect in the law taught us that.

Only the Spirit transforming information into knowledge can do that. That's what revelation is. It's the process by which the

Spirit takes hold of the things we're learning and plants them deep within our souls, where they can germinate and bear godly fruit. Without slowing and thinning in our lives, without enough space to stop and allow that process to take place, we'll be stuck learning about God but never knowing Him.

It's possible for even the simplest person to become the wisest through constant time in God's presence, but it's not possible for the wisest, most well-read person to enter the kingdom of God without prayer.

Becoming a beholding people is as much about the process of decluttering as it is about building a life of proactive prayer, because all this noise clogs our spiritual sight, and we can't see much through foggy lenses. We could think of this as our two hands of prayer—one clearing a path for God, the other reaching out toward Him in communion.

It's always wise to start the hardest journeys simply and small. Radical overnight purges generally don't last for long, and the last thing we need is more spiritual crash diets. Pioneering a clear life takes time, thoughtfulness, and compassion-receiving. We're born into an immense swell of noise, entertainment addiction, and gluttony. It's going to take some time to confront the tsunami.

So often the spiritual blankness we feel when we think about God is due to our blankness in general because we spend so little time with ourselves apart from the noise of life. Then, because we don't know any better, we project that onto God and make it His fault that we can't hear or sense Him. I know this is painfully true of me, especially in these times, and I sense God's deep compassion for us in this very full world we inhabit.

Many of our greatest challenges in our spiritual lives aren't so much about what we are doing in our prayer lives but about what we're doing outside them. So, living a life of beholding is as much about choosing what we don't do as it is about what we do. Maybe even more so.

This, to me, is part of what it means to pray without ceasing. It is to see our every moment as divine connection, looking to shed whatever noise we can to see that truth more clearly and making our hearts as attentive as possible to heaven whilst we do the ordinary things. By unnoising, we create a life in which it's more natural to behold God.

BOREDOM

Boredom is a human right. As a musician and writer, I can honestly say that many of my best ideas and works have come from the most boring days, weeks, and moments of my life. Boredom gives us time and space to think about things that we otherwise would never think about. It allows our minds to trail off into weird places and our imaginations to generate whole new worlds and alternative futures.

The only way for us to reach those little frontiers of our often-crowded minds is to allow enough mental space to first confront, process, and find closure on whatever consumes us at present—stressful work situations, a tricky relationship, some life-admin—and to then drift off into the imaginative ether.

Bizarrely, to be bored today, one must be highly motivated. It's far easier to read the news on the toilet, listen to a podcast whilst you walk, take the highway instead of the scenic route, pick up a book, organize another coffee, clean the house, catch up on work, or do whatever else may be your boredom slayer of choice. What person in their right mind would ever *choose* to be bored? Beholders, if you ask me.

To be bored, we have to clear copious amounts of space in our lives through the little moments that gather around us in our between-things minutes. In other words, it's the decision to not listen to the radio in traffic, to not check social media on our toilet break, and to just sit and stare out a window during the sunset or a rainy night instead of watching a movie.

The opportunity of boredom arrives at any moment where our first reaction is to reach for our phones, food, or some other stimulant of choice. Not doing those things gives us time to be gripped by God or at the least to notice the world and ourselves within it.

Boredom is a prerequisite for a beholding life because it's a good sign we've finally got to the end of overworking and ignoring ourselves and are open enough to be surprised by whatever happens next. When we're bored, it's because we've finally made enough space to think about what we need to before reaching the wide horizon of "other stuff" our minds wander into when they don't have another urgent appointment.

Being bored is choosing to believe that if we create enough of that space and direct it toward the Spirit within us, we'll hear God around the questions we have as well as those we've never even thought to ask. We were made to be bored; it's a human right, and I think we need a revolution to bring it back into fashion.

Boredom, slowing, and thinning are practices we can build into our lives to help create stillness within us, and it's stillness that we're really reaching for with all this. Orthodox Bishop Kallistos Ware tells us that "stillness is a state of inner tranquility or mental quietude and concentration. Not simply silence, but an attitude, of listening to God and of an openness to God."[37] It helps us keep attentive to God.

We can't sit and practise stillness in the quiet of our rooms in the morning and then go about our days mindlessly and hope we can keep attentive to God's presence in our lives. But we also can't rely on the world to calm down for us. We must do what we can with our schedules and the noise around us, and slowly build stillness and attentiveness within us through slowing, thinning, and a healthy dose of boredom.

PRAYER IS A BANQUET

Prayer is ultimately about union between us and God, but in the same way we don't learn to swim by jumping into the deep end, that union is often grown through a lifetime of gradual, inch-by-inch, daily acts of devotional love. To grow a life of beholding like that, we need to grow our repertoire of prayer.

We can think of it like training at the gym. To have a well-rounded, healthy body, a workout routine will include different exercises for the upper and lower body. It will include some cardio and stretches too. People tend to love some exercises more than others. Most don't like leg days, for example. But in Aotearoa we have a name for guys who are all upper-body muscle and don't do the work below; we call them "chicken legs."

We don't want spiritual chicken legs. Some forms of prayer we'll love more than others, and each of us is naturally inclined toward a particular kind. But practising other forms of prayer that don't come naturally to us grows us in powerful ways too. I'm not saying our prayer lives should be full of hard work and stuff we don't enjoy. But I've always felt we should do mostly what we love with a little of what stretches us.

Many of the spiritual practices that grow a beholding life, as it turns out, are centred on a more human way of experiencing the world. They're re-earthing. Things like silence and solitude are just as much basic human needs as anything else, but that doesn't mean they're not prayerful too. We are organic beings made to operate in a particular way of life that has become foreign to many of us. Reclaiming that way of life has an important role to play in prayer.

Living a life full of the practices of beholding doesn't necessarily make a beholding life either; they must be filled with God and a deep desire for Him. Plenty of communities have been amazing at prayerful dedication but still miss God. The religious leaders of Jesus' time were committed pray-ers, but they totally missed God's presence among them.

We need to show up to prayer practices with faithful expectation that God is there, He loves us, and He longs to and will commune with us in that space. Those last few points are crucial. Prayer requires faith. The practices in themselves aren't the point, but they are as important to a life of prayer as scales are to musicians.

If we're to become a people of beholding-communion, we need a wide view of prayer and the ways we engage God, because different ways of sitting with God offer us different ways of experiencing Him. That goes for all the various kinds of prayer practices those different traditions give us.

Sadly, a lot of beauty has fallen through the cracks because of the prejudice our traditions have inadvertently taught us, and we miss out when we assume that a form of prayer foreign to us is either wrong or restrictive. In my experience, it's not the form or type of prayer that limits a person, but the energy, life, and faith the person fills the prayer with. A little faith goes a long way.

As Christians, we have a vast history of prayer to explore to build a wide and full life of union with our Father. Prayer, for Christians, isn't so much a set menu as it is a vast and invitational banquet.

Unfortunately, many of us have siloed ourselves in our own particular tradition, often desperately needing a safe, practical boundary to outwork our lives with God. Traditional churches can be skeptical of extemporaneous and charismatic prayer, assuming it's all hype and emotion, and charismatic churches can be prone to seeing liturgy, read prayer, and contemplation as too passive or rigid for God to fill.

This prejudice has led to real spiritual malnourishment in our communities and often to imbalanced Christians. We have so much to learn from each other; a beholding disposition lends to seeing and celebrating that and the adventure it offers us. Prayer, because it's solely centred on our affection, desire, and love for God, is a powerful way to bring the church together. Sharing one another's forms of prayer may just open a wedge in the door for church unity that few other things can.

I was lucky in that I stumbled into many contemplative practices not through being taught technique or reading books but through having my life turned upside down from chronic illness. I say *lucky* because I was the kind of person who was largely very prejudiced and skeptical of other traditions. Especially those focused on contemplative practices. God knew I'd need a life lesson, not a lecture, to have my prayer life transformed.

The added benefit to stumbling into this new way of prayer was that no one told me it was an either-or option. During the years when stillness, silence, and liturgy became a treasure to me, I was still singing my lungs out at charismatic worship nights, speaking in tongues, and laying hands on friends at church to hear words from God and to pray for healing and breakthrough.

It never occurred to me that the charismatic and contemplative practices might be opposing forces. It was all the Spirit, leading me into God's heart in both new ways and old ways. We create those kinds of distinctions; God doesn't. Contemplative practices have done nothing but inspire and reinforce my seeking God's dynamic and active presence in my life. They haven't at all made me more "religious" or "boring." Being charismatic isn't a personality type; it's a belief that God's gifts for the church, and His desire to act in the world, are as real today as ever.

Sharing one another's forms of prayer may just open a wedge in the door for church unity that few other things can.

If we allow it to, a life of beholding can make room for a banquet of forms of prayer that includes traditional and charismatic, Protestant and Eastern Orthodox, Pentecostal and Methodist. We can see beholding in charismatic worship gatherings, discover it in the silence of the Quakers or the liturgy of Catholicism.

In a beholding spirituality, Celtic poetry inspires a new awareness in us, and the arts find their place embracing the tension between certainty and sense. Because we're recentring our values on love, fruits, and the dignity of all people, a beholding generation has the potential to heal interchurch wounds and celebrate what they otherwise couldn't celebrate in the past.

The church has engaged in so many rich and deep prayerful practices for centuries. A brief survey will detail sabbath, solitude, fasting, praying the hours, the prayer of examen, *lectio divina*, liturgies for morning and evening, and the Jesus Prayer. Not to mention the gathered community on Sundays with their worship, prayer, word, and sacrament.

Then there are sung worship nights, intercessory free-prayer gatherings, and praying for the sick, possessed, and lonely. Add inner-healing prayer, prayer retreats, and prophetic prayer where we seek to hear God's voice for others.

To cover all the various kinds of prayer, both historical and recent, would take another whole book, a book far better written by someone steeped in their history and practice, of which there are many.

We don't have to reject one tradition in favour of another. Opening up a banquet of prayer means we can celebrate liturgy and charismatic prayer in the same faith. I encourage you to explore the banquet of prayer the church has to offer and try them out. Whatever you decide, if you do it as a lover and not a professional, you'll notice the technique matters less anyway. You may find that silent retreats are just what your highly active, loud church has been hankering for. Or extended sung worship nights might bring about a new deep desire for new experiences of God.

I know for me, learning to practise silence throughout my day was a game changer, as have been the morning and evening devotions in the New Zealand Prayer Book when my spiritual life feels dry and I'm out of words of my own. When I've had the privilege of attending Catholic mass or participating in Anglican prayer nights, I've been as deeply enriched as when I've wept my way through free-flowing sung worship at church on Sunday.

Knowing, loving, and experiencing God is the one common thing we have as Christians. Maybe in that way, prayer can bring us together as we never thought possible. If we'll only open our spiritual stomachs to the banquet our diversity offers.

Building a prayer life is about one thing: a lived and continuous experience of the wonder that is God. But it won't happen spontaneously or by accident. At least not in a lifetime. To create a life of communion, we need to slowly build habits into our lives that draw us nearer to Him.

In the chaotic and noisy world we live in, it begins with clearing the way and making room for God. Not only so He can speak, but so we can be the kind of people who hear. So much of our spiritual wilderness, I believe, is our tendency to live a busy, noisy life, then expect God to show up big in the few moments we give Him. He'll do that at times because He loves us and is kind beyond words, but for us to grow in communion with Him, we'll need to slow down, thin out our lives, and grow in inner stillness.

Thankfully, there are practices to help us do that. Practices that the church has employed for millennia. One of these has a unique power in building a beholding life. A practice so offensive to our world that it's as much a revolution as an invitation from God: *silence*.

Chapter 9

SILENCE, IT'S GOD'S LANGUAGE

*"You, Holy Spirit, are a whisper. A frequency
so humble that our city noise would drown You
out but for desperately longing hearts."*

Prayer Vol. 01

*"When I listen,
when I let You start the conversation,
all my questions disintegrate into affection."*

Prayer Vol. 02

*"The LORD is in his holy temple; let all the
earth be silent before him."*[38]

Silence draws us into the reality that God is. Is near us, is for us,
is with us. Is.

The sun rises in silence, gravity pushes and pulls in it. The stars light the sky in silence, and under the soil of the earth, life sprouts from seedlings amidst it. Oxygen gives life to our cells beyond our listening ear, and the greatest of all, love itself, lives largely inaudible in the hearts and minds of its keepers.

Silence is the language of some of the grandest miracles in creation, showing us a little of what it's like to stand before the even more magnificent God, quietly. God is Spirit, and though none of us have seen Him,[39] we can at least assume that a spirit doesn't have a physical mouth or a voice box any more than our own inner self does. Made in His image, we've been equipped with the ability to communicate without sound through our eyes or a knowing embrace. Silence speaks.

There are two kinds of silence: external and internal. The practice of silence in prayer, though it often starts out in the external shape, is really a doorway into an internal way of being. Silence is a way of being before God in our entire lives; it's a disposition. To get there, we need to practise thinning out the noise in our lives, as we've already explored, and focusing our bodies and senses in deliberate times with God.

Most of how we make sense of the world is from this internal silence, or darkness, within us. Not darkness as in evil or bad, but as in a mystery. The deepest places of the ocean are the darkest and hardest to reach, and the most distant stars shine most clearly on the darkest nights, but that doesn't make either sinister or unholy. So it is with God. As the psalmist tells us, God has "made darkness his secret place."[40]

Inner silence invites us to dive into that mystery and cohabitate with it. It's about embracing unspokenness and meeting with God in the quietness that can be found in so much of our lives. It's more expansive than thinking, but more engaged than emptying ourselves out into nothing. It's an intentional journey into God.

Our emotions, for example, are strangely quiet, they're a different language. Emotions don't *tell* us what they're feeling, they *show* us. They just appear out of nowhere and drive us to an action or belief. We don't question the power of emotions, we accept them as totally normal and natural. Yet many of us struggle to accept the movements of God in a similar way, becoming aware somehow of His life within us speaking without words.

One of the great gifts of walking with God over time is the fine-tuning of this listening to the silence of God within us. But it takes our quieting down ourselves enough to discover it.

So being silent before God in our own personal prayer times isn't wasteful, it's recalibrating, quieting us for a little while so we can learn this other language and what it's like to speak in the divine tongue. It's in this kind of silence that we learn to be like God, becoming present listeners. Silence is critical to prayer because it's hard to let God be when we're incessantly talking externally and internally. We have to look out from all of that to where He is, quiet in the world around us. Doing what He does.

In silence we allow the noise of life, and of our minds, to sink to the bottom of us like sediment in a river so we can see with greater clarity the Spirit within and around us. It is, like Sabbath, a humility act. It gives God the opportunity to be the first speaker, and in this way like listening and watching prayer, is deeply prophetic. It allows us to follow God's lead rather than our own agenda.

Silence is about acknowledging that God is speaking and is actively and creatively engaging with us through our mind, body, and the world surrounding us, but it's up to us to tune in. How we bring ourselves to it is important.

It took me a long time to learn how to bring myself to silence. I was spending almost all day, every day, in solitude and silence because of my health, but that didn't necessarily make it quality time. It's very possible to live quietly but not in inner silence with God. My life may have been quiet, but my insides were in total anguish.

One day the thought dawned on me that maybe all this "useless" time being too unwell to work was an opportunity to learn how to pray, and so I started showing up to it. I began paying attention to the silence that already naturally existed. Stilling myself internally, inviting God to speak. Just that very act of turning toward silence and inviting it into communion transformed it. It redeemed in my soul what my sickness tried to steal. It returned me beauty for ashes.

In the same way, silence can also be a disposition as we work, intentionally bringing ourselves to it with that same stillness inside, rather than rushing through whatever we need to do. When you think about the normal rhythms of our days, we actually encounter a lot of natural silence. Times of quiet fill our eating, driving, evenings, going to bed, waking, walking, or even waiting in line at shops.

Silence surrounds us, but we often just pass through those moments mindlessly, or at least unintentionally, like I was. The practice of inner silence is about seeing those spaces as invitations and intentionally bringing ourselves to them with, or before, God.

THE POWER OF NOISE

Scientists have discovered that audible noise pollution in the world today is so pervasive that it's having a powerful, negative neurological impact. At the time of this writing, studies by the World Health Organization suggest that noise leads to 12,000 premature deaths a year, 22 million cases of chronic annoyance, and 6.5 million cases of chronic high sleep disturbance in Europe alone. It causes learning impairments in children when schools are close to airports and is labeled by the WHO as the largest environmental cause of health problems after air pollution.[41]

It would be fair to say that noise is having a major impact on our physical and mental lives and, in itself, deserves a counterbalance if and wherever possible. At the least, removing the ambient noise of radio, TV, podcasts, and raised voices in our lives is a place to start.

But physical noise isn't the only kind of sound on the offensive today. We are surrounded by an overwhelming volume of information, opinion, and entertainment. Where it was once relatively natural for a person to spend ample time processing their inner life, now it's almost an impossibility without real discipline. With our phones on standby, we rarely wait in a line, go for a walk, or even sit in traffic without checking the news or social media.

Whereas in monasteries nuns and monks eat, work, and rest together in silence, it's likely you and I need to tune out of attention-seeking technologies and learn to manage the competing voices and opinions within ourselves. To discover that we have a voice of our own in the first place, let alone God's as well.

Sadly, the lack of self-knowledge this causes skews our understanding of God, the world, and others and inhibits us from discerning the difference between them. Our inner lives, like chores, can only be put off for so long before the mess overwhelms us. Without space, without silence, we find ourselves quickly overwhelmed when we finally *do* turn inward to face the mounting chaos. An overwhelm that is seriously contributing to the anxiety many experience in the world today. In light of this, silence is really a humanising practice. One which is important for clearing the way to know God.

CREATING SILENT RHYTHMS

Individually, silence can be practised when and however best suits the rhythms and realities of our days. Personally, I would recommend searching for a local retreat centre or monastery that offers day or weekend silent retreats and start there. The benefit of experiencing retreat silence is that you can see how others do it and even have guides close by who can help you make sense of what you're feeling. In my early days of this practice, I found those larger chunks really energising. You might even consider booking two or three single-day silent retreats a year as a spiritual staple.

Outside of those more formal and extended periods of silence, though, choosing a time and place you can practise every day is the best way to grow—even if it's only five minutes initially. My mind is prone to wander, so I've discovered sitting in front of a lit candle really helps me—especially at night when the lights are dim and the body is tired! Both because the candle reminds me of the Holy Spirit and His life within me, and because it's a moving, living thing to focus on.

Once you start practising a moment in the morning or evening like this, you'll find interest building within you for more. As that happens, try exercising without earbuds, driving without listening to a podcast, leaving your phone in the car during meetings or when you're shopping, or picking a daily chore to lock into. You'll notice those moments slowly and more naturally being filled with an awareness of God.

Silence is really a humanising practice. One which is important for clearing the way to know God.

During a time when I was doing lots of meetings with people out around the city, I would arrive five to ten minutes early, park, and take the time to sit in silence before God. Now when all my kids are in bed, I sit in my chair, close my eyes, and sit with God before I pick up anything else. I find if I do it at that moment, it stops me drifting off into tech use, slows me down, and changes the course of my evening. All to say, the more of these little moments you build into your life, the more you'll sit in them constantly as an internal way of being rather than a set of practices.

SILENCE, TOGETHER

To practise times of daily silence like this is a revolution against the Attention Economy of our time. It's radical like that. But doing it together can also create a haven in a world full of violent voices. My favorite prayer meetings over the years have slowly become the ones that start in silence—even the charismatic ones. It often changes the direction and tone of the group. It settles us.

Gathering your small group, prayer group, or church community for evenings of shared silence can have a profound effect. Plenty of people at church don't turn up to prayer meetings because they're shy or don't know what to say. But a profound unity that's hard to explain gathers in a room when people are silent together in God. It runs deep.

Vigils at times of death and candlelit Good Friday gatherings are also powerful when held in silence. Even spending thirty or forty minutes together in silence midweek before work will have a surprising effect on you and your community's life of beholding.

Imagine a world where church communities could become harbours for noise refugees: people exhausted and burnt out not only by the noise pollution of our world but also by the social and political noise, such as never-ending opinions of hatred, anger, and accusation that have become the norm in our culture.

What if church communities were known again for providing candlelit, aesthetic spaces open to tired and exhausted people during the week just to provide some respite? Or if silence was practised in a reconciling way by allowing the hurt, offended, and angry to share their pain whilst we silently listen? Not with the intent of responding or justifying, but simply as a sacred act of love? What if we protested in silence in the public space against the injustices of our time, showing solidarity whilst offering a sign of the age to come in the process?

It's difficult to fault gentle opposition, and silence can be shockingly confronting. I can see a world in which silence is so rare, and listening such an endangered species, that a Christian community that practises patient waiting and graceful silence would become the light on the hill of our cities again.

At this moment, as I write this, Christian opinion and voice feel louder than ever, and in some ways that's great, we should absolutely have something to say about the injustices of our world. I'm certainly not advocating for silence in the face of destructive and oppressive systems in the world. But we can also cross a line where we begin believing that talk alone can bring the kind of change that Christ promises will only come through the power of another kingdom altogether: His kingdom.

Silence helps keep us balanced. When we're silent before God, the stones of our frustrations, disappointments, and anger with others have time to sink to the bottom of the lake so the water can become a little clearer before we speak. As a patience builder, the practice of silence may help the church become a little softer in the face of harsh criticism and division. It may help us show the world another language.

Silence isn't about denial or lack; it's about a radical embodiment of another more subversive way. A way that makes more room for God's voice than our own. It demonstrates a quiet resolution to let God be louder than we are, and to let prayer have a greater effect than opinion. It's about creating lives and communities where the world can retreat from the violence of words and opinions, rather than attempting to fight with the same weapons of power, aggression, and accusation that the world uses.

Becoming silent communities—places where silence is practised communally when we meet—also helps us to become a more prophetic people. I've noticed people who don't consider themselves able to hear God's voice become strangely revelatory when they're offered the space to listen. For those who are surrounded by great pray-ers, some can feel at a loss for words and eloquence, but when they share a room in silent prayer, they often have something to offer in conversation afterwards.

When I've practised silence for five minutes or so in the beginning of communal free-prayer meetings, it gave those of us gathered ample time to let what we *thought* God might be saying, or what we *thought* He wanted us to pray, to dissipate so we could then pray with Christ for what He really longed to address in that moment. People would almost always pray more restedly in those gatherings, from a place of intimacy and witness rather than separation and angst.

That was profound for me. The silence made us more aware of God, and that awareness changed our agenda. We were magnetised to closeness. Then, when the energy left the room, the same silence returned, and no one felt the need to fill it with empty prayers or harder work. We were rested, real, honest. I loved that.

What if during our gatherings in the week or on the weekend we began with silence, a time for those coming to allow the noise of the world to settle, so that we reached out into God together from a place of rest and peace rather than noise and urgency? What if in practising silence together in this way we taught others how to make more room for themselves, their inner lives, and the life of the Spirit within them, and in doing so helped them discover new empathy, kindness, slowness, and divine creativity? Silent communities are beholding communities, and beholding communities make more room for the radical transformation that only God can bring.

THE PRACTICE OF SILENCE

So how do we practise silence, exactly? In a methodical sense, it's simple. We make regular space in our day to sit before God without saying anything, reading anything, or expecting anything other than giving our attention to Him. We could do this three times a day for three minutes, for twenty minutes in the morning before we get up for the day, whilst we're sitting in bed with our coffee in hand, or at the end of the day before a lit candle. We could do this at a day or weekend retreat or by taking a morning to walk in nature.

All of these are great ways to practise quietness with God, but each of us will approach it differently depending on who we are and the kind of life we live. I've found that the practical element isn't so much the challenge; it's the internal aspect that often makes silence difficult to abide in. It's coming before God without agenda with the specific intention of allowing Him to hold the room.

Stilling ourselves like this has a way of drawing out our internal mess we haven't processed, or at least are struggling to. For anxious or depressed people, silence can be the loudest moments of our days; for the lonely, it can be stabbing. The longer it's been since we've built silence as a rhythm into our lives, the more punctuated those challenges may feel. If anxiety and depression are part of your journey, begin lightly, give yourself grace, and ask a trusted, mature Christian friend to journey with you. Silence isn't meant to be loneliness.

The art of it is how we handle the tremors that come from within when we finally turn down the volume in a noisy and anxious world. That we experience those moments is evidence of its importance. Evidence that God is at work.

And don't worry, you're not alone. Everyone who has ever built this practice into their life has had to face these challenges in order to grow. When I lead silent retreats, some people have panic experiences within the first hour of a day-long stretch, but they always make it through, grateful they pushed on. As we begin, I warn the group about it, tell them it may come, and invite them to kindly inquire of themselves where and why those feelings and emotions have come knocking.

The important thing is to pay attention to those thoughts and feelings that come and bring them honestly to God. What's really going on is you're noticing what's under the hood, and that's great news. The practice of silence is about recognising all of that and learning how to bring it to God when it comes. It's called being human.

At some point, humanity spent ample time in silence; it wasn't a separate-life practice. It was a home for us. Today, it's more of a holiday destination, and we need to have some grace with ourselves and others in acclimatising to it as a regular part of our lives. It's not going to feel natural to most of us at the start, and that's okay. But refusing to build it into our lives due to the discomfort it can bring us only prolongs the fundamental issue. We will still carry all of it within us, and what is left unaddressed will continue to wreak havoc with our vulnerability and openness with God.

Another important encouragement is not to fret distraction. The best thing to do when distraction comes is to simply acknowledge it and either hold it before God or return to a centring practice. (We'll get to that in a minute.) Distractions are normal, and if you're coming from a noisy visual-audio world of social media, podcasts, YouTube, and video consumption, your brain will be hardwired to think in two- to six-second bits. Sitting down and trying to turn it off won't suddenly change that; you'll need to retrain it like you would a muscle.

It's also important to remember that we're not trying to empty ourselves out. The Word became flesh, a human being in a body, and there's no reason we need to start trying to be anything different from how we were created. In silence and contemplation, we awaken to the reality of God within us, coming to us in our normal, ordinary lives. We're not attempting to exit ourselves to find Him.

Distraction can sometimes be a way the Holy Spirit nods at an issue that is keeping us from Him. When thoughts come to mind when I'm in silence, I say, "Father, if this is You, let the seed take to soil and grow. Speak to it, and show me Your heart. If it's not You, let it fall away so that I can be with You in the here and now." Thoughts aren't a problem. We're not trying to be blank. We're showing up to God, and that means He will sometimes speak to us through our thoughts.

At some point, humanity spent ample time in silence;
it wasn't a separate-life practice. It was a home for us.

If you're just busy minded, that's okay too. Some days are harder than others, especially at the start. Simply acknowledge it and see your decision to stay before God, and centre yourself on Him as an act of stubborn love and sacrifice. Remember, beholding isn't always about feeling or having an "experience"; it's about making room for God however He may be with us in that time and place. No matter what happens, if we give it to Him with longing, our time will bear the fruit of God.

It took me becoming unwell to give God enough space to be heard. Before that, prayer was mostly me speaking at length with a little bit of listening time. I tended to crowd the room. Then, when I got sick and spent countless hours quiet and alone, I didn't show up to it as if it was an invitation to deeper divine communion. I allowed my inner noise to run wild within me.

It took me months to start seeing that time as an opportunity to listen. To allow my understanding of prayer to be reshaped.

Sometimes silence is just that, the art of accepting the season brought upon us by pandemics, accidents, or job loss as a holy opportunity, not only a death of some kind. To do that we need to consciously show up to God in the vacuum of what was. Being willing to see an invitation to prayer arriving to us in the shape of our lives.

Whilst they're in silence, many people like to practise centring words or breathing prayer to help them stay in the moment.

Centring

Centring is the practice of choosing a word and kindly bringing your focus back by speaking it internally every time your mind wanders. This word can be anything, but it's helpful to choose something that builds intimacy and awareness with God. Some suggestions could be *God, love, Spirit, peace, rest, sin, grace,* or *kindness.* During silence it's important to receive God's compassion for our often-tumultuous mind and internal condition. When you feel your mind wander, don't be frustrated or angry; give it permission to do so. Then calmly and quietly repeat your centring word to realign your focus on God.

Breathing

Another helpful practice is to focus on your breathing. As you notice the rhythm of your breath and lungs, choose two words to repeat as you inhale and exhale. These could be *Spirit come, Jesus Christ, Holy Spirit, Divine Love,* or *grace peace.* It's important for them to be words that foster intimacy and awareness between you and God. Then, like the centring prayer, if you notice your mind wandering (which you will!), gently bring your focus back onto God with your breathing and inhale-exhale words again.

Remember, silence as a practice takes time. When most of us begin practising daily silence, we don't believe we receive much from it. It can feel like a wrestle for ten or twenty minutes, and we may even come away feeling more exhausted than when we began. But persist. No one feels great after their first run of the season; the body takes time to adjust, and so do we with silence. Practise receiving this love that will change you by awakening you to God as you sit with Him, rebelling against a world that vies for your every thought.

Whatever your struggle and however hard, keep turning up and giving God the space. Over time you'll feel yourself slide into God-awareness more and more quickly as it becomes spiritual muscle memory for you. You'll even find that before long you're disappointed when your time is over. You'll want to sit there for hours.

You'll also notice that over time you'll realise silence comes to you in the midst of your workday, whilst you're waiting in line somewhere, or even at a party. The regular practice of silence causes it to leak out everywhere, slowing down your internal world even in the midst of whatever life you're living.

The world we live in is noisy, and noisy in a way that becomes reflected in our internal lives as well. But God doesn't tend to try to compete with our high-volume lives. He waits. Waits for us to take the time to settle down and listen for Him within us, where He lives. Regularly practising silence in our daily routine, and intentionally showing up to it, is a powerful way to hold God before us in all things—to train ourselves in the quiet language of God.

Chapter 10

LEARNING TO WATCH & LISTEN

"You're praying before I am, God—
I'm simply joining the conversation."

Prayer Vol. 02

"Father, teach me presentness
as prayer."

Prayer Vol. 02

"Keep your eyes open for GOD, watch for his
works; be alert for signs of his presence."[42]

In beholding prayer we're learning to be the second actor. That means that our intercession, seeking God for things and conversation, begins with His heart and flows from the rested power that comes from allowing Him to lead. But when it comes to letting

God lead, how we think about watching and listening often needs to change.

Because we're so used to a world of people with physical mouths, ears, and eyes, we tend to subconsciously project onto God our human appendages, expecting Him to respond to us in the same way we would to each other. This used to really frustrate me. I would wonder why God didn't just speak in an audible voice or manifest physically when it seemed obvious that would be by far the most productive way for us to get to know each other.

But really what I was doing was equivalent to demanding that someone from another culture speak my language, on my terms. Except with God, it's not just a language I'm demanding He speak, but a different communication style altogether. God is loving and kind, and He reaches out to us in ways we can understand; Jesus is the perfect example of that. But it's also upon us to learn His language and to discover His ways of communing.

God dwells within us. He is Spirit, and as a result, He speaks to us and communes with us in Spirit, His language. Jesus said, "Anyone who loves me will obey my teaching. My Father will love them, and we will come to them and make our home with them."[43] God's home is within us, so He doesn't need to use an external audible voice any more than we do when we're processing something internally.

We're still watching for and listening to God, but what we mean by those two dispositions is vastly different from how we usually experience them.

Learning to speak this language is a lot like being a child again. Maybe this is what Jesus meant when He said, "No one can see the kingdom of God unless they are born again."[44] We're literally learning a new language through an entirely different means than what we were first born with.

We're like babies again who have to learn the sound of their own parents' voices, their body language, their spoken language, and the different things their voice inflections mean. But this time it's with a Spirit who precedes creation, lives outside of time, is all-powerful, and has a knowledge expanse that we will never touch the sides of. Our being born again is a communication recalibration like no other. The good news is this means we can have some grace on ourselves (and others!).

Although receiving God is instant, learning to commune, hear, see, and understand the God who lives in us will take the rest of our lives. We may feel frustrated with our own journey of watching and listening to God. But if it takes us years to grow the ability to harness human language, understand human social cues, and relate to other human people, though we're surrounded by their physical presence 24/7 and have thousands of years of cultural history to lean on, how much more will it take us to learn to hear and see the invisible God who few even seek to find? This is an invitation to an adventurous faith, not a roadblock. Though I admit, it would be much nicer to receive a Matrix-style download at baptism!

Throughout my discovering journey of beholding, I've identified three forms of prayer that have helped me to grow in learning to understand God's language: listening, watching, and prophetic.

LISTENING PRAYER

One of my greatest personal lessons through these years of learning to behold God, because it used to feel so unnatural to me, is the practice of listening.

Listening prayer is premised on the fact that God's promise to hear us is constant, and He is the best listener we know. The psalmist tells us that our Father always has an ear to our lives, listening to every detail: "You have searched me, LORD, and you know me. You know when I sit and when I rise; you perceive my thoughts from afar. You discern my going out and my lying down; you are familiar with all my ways. Before a word is on my tongue you, LORD, know it completely."[45] God is a fantastic listener.

When God listens, He's attentive to our every word and not with an eye for critical analysis, but in kindness and care as the psalmist said in 86:15: "But you, Lord, are a compassionate and gracious God, slow to anger, abounding in love and faithfulness." In listening prayer, we can express our heart's highs, lows, and everything in between to God with a faith that expects His kind attentiveness, regardless of whether we feel it or not.

Listening prayer is first a deep-seated conviction that God *is* listening to us. But there's more to it. We can be the same for God.

When we listen to God with this same attentiveness, prayer becomes not just a place to receive answers about things, but a place to learn to feel what He does. To know Him by seating ourselves *in* Him. That could be an emotional experience, but it doesn't have to be. It's about paying attention to God in an engulfing way, with our whole being, allowing who God is and what's on His heart to fill us.

Receiving God is instant; learning to commune,
hear, see, and understand the God who lives
in us will take the rest of our lives.

It's not about words or exchange but about an abiding, engulfing knowing. This kind of listening is about hearing in our bellies and knowing in our bones God's celebration, grief, excitement, or hope for another, ourselves, or for the world. In the same way a hug can say more about love and withness than service or actions, so listening prayer receives God as a person who is alive to all things and feels them as we do, but in His perfect love and hope.

When we practise this kind of prayer, we also learn how to replicate God's incredible listening disposition to the world around us. As we feel what God feels, as we sit with Him in answerless affection, we grow the muscles we need for empathy in the world around us.

A generation that beholds God through listening prayer secretly practises the muscles needed to learn to sit with others, their enemies, those they don't understand, or friends with polar political views. It decimates personal loneliness because it assumes and trusts that God is there even when He's saying nothing. As we come to experience that we're not alone ourselves, we're able to show others what it's like to feel that same withness from personal experience.

When it comes to listening to God, we take our lead from God. He is the first and best listener and for millennia has been listening even to those who don't understand Him and can't see the world as He does. There is no one on earth more practised in patient-listening than God Himself. At any given moment He is listening to almost 8 billion of us (not counting the dead!).

Scripture is full of examples of God listening to His people and even being attentive to the poor, the proud, or creation herself. We don't often talk about God being the best listener, but He is never not listening to you and me.

GOD SITS WITH US

Henri Nouwen made a profound statement about the power of listening in his book *Out of Solitude*:

> When we honestly ask ourselves which persons in our lives mean the most to us, we often find that it is those who, instead of giving much advice, solutions, or cures, have chosen rather to share our pain and touch our wounds with a warm and tender hand. The friend who can be silent with us in a moment of despair or confusion, who can stay with us in an hour of grief or bereavement, who can tolerate not knowing, not curing, not healing and face with us the reality of our powerlessness, that is the friend who cares.[46]

When I read this for the first time, it was like someone giving expression to an unacknowledged but deeply believed truth within me. I've always felt more understood and heard by those who have sat with me, rather than spoken to me, during all these years of ongoing illness. It's also entirely true of how I've come to understand God.

God is the friend who listens and cares, not just with factual intent, but with compassion. Though we may not emotionally feel it, when we pour out our souls to God, His silence isn't distance or disconnection, it's empathetic love expressing itself in something far more important and powerful than words: withness. God is communing with us through His silent response, becoming not the friend who offers easy answers or trite advice, but the friend who realises that sometimes it's more important to be seen and heard than answered. Even when we ourselves don't understand it.

In his book *Anatomy of the Soul*, psychologist Curt Thompson referenced work done by Daniel Siegel about compassionate listening:

> An important part of how people change—not just their experiences, but also their brains—is through the process of telling their stories to an empathetic listener. When a person tells her story and is truly heard and understood, both she and the listener undergo actual changes in their brain circuitry. They feel a greater sense of emotional and relational connection, decreased anxiety, and greater awareness of and compassion for others' suffering.[47]

In other words, we're hardwired to be listened to with empathy, not just heard. When God listens to us, when we believe God truly hears us in this way, our brains change shape and we become the very kinds of people we believe God is. Our physical makeup is literally rewired to grasp love better.

Without a firm belief that God cares, and that He's present every time we groan within or through words, we won't receive the transformation He's offering us in love. Our part is to trust He listens and cares, His is to do the deep work as we speak. As we allow Him to bring this transformation to us through communion, we'll be able to turn and face the world around us with that same empathetic listening love. Eventually, this transforming empathy learned in prayer transforms every other life around us.

Our listening to God in prayer has to be premised in the way God listens. If we can learn to see God this way, not only will we gain the energy we need to become this kind of listener to others in the world around us, but we'll be able to give back to God what He gives to us—we will become empathetic listeners of Him too.

For me, this is practising listening prayer: coming into awareness of God with the intention of hearing and participating in His heart with a spirit of withness.

Isn't that what prophetic prayer and intercession really are? Isn't it the ability to hear God and allow that listening to transform our very being so it pours out of us in our prayer lives and actions toward the world? I wonder if we often miss out on deeper communion with God because we assume it's our role to speak and it's His role to listen and respond, rather than the other way around.

Every relationship is built on mutual listening, including our relationship with God. Our friendship is not just about business, not just about getting things done, but sharing our hearts as one another's beloved.

Listening like this involves far more than just cognitive attention; it requires opening ourselves up to receive God within us in a way that allows what He's saying to be felt and born in our very own souls. It requires that we let down our walls and be willing to feel.

Similar to when our close friends share the exciting news that they're having a baby or just got the promotion of their dreams, they're not looking for a factual pat on the back, they're looking for us to jump with excitement with them, to share in it. They want to see our face light up and experience the very joy they're experiencing.

There's something about sharing our experiences, really sharing them, that strengthens our bonds and helps us to not only feel seen but to contribute joy and life to our world. It's no different with God. God isn't looking to download information to us like robots; He wants us to jump with joy as He does, to celebrate with Him, to feel the love He has for us and others, and even to grieve for the world like He does. He wants us to be like Him.

With listening prayer, we can either wait for God to reveal His heart to us or proactively bring something before Him in a listening manner. In the former, we allow Him to start the conversation where He longs to. In the latter, we allow Him to guide our understanding of a situation, person, or need. In both cases, though, the emphasis is on receiving the whole of God into us.

THE PRACTICE OF LISTENING

Listening prayer can be undertaken in any way that you feel most open to God. If it's helpful to you, here's how I practise it.

I find a comfortable space where I can be alone with God without interruption or distraction. Then I open up my heart to Him. I do this by imagining there is a door in my chest that leads to my innermost being. I picture myself opening that door and the flood of God's light pouring in to dwell with me there. Of course, God is already there within me, but this is my way of more consciously inviting Him.

Often, I sense and become aware of God within me, communing there, an agenda-nakedness of sorts where neither of us is hiding anything of ourselves from each other. A place of mutual seenness. Most times, I find that the degree to which I allow God to see me is the degree to which I'm able to really see Him. One way to do this is to hold all my mess, frustration, or whatever else I'm feeling at the time in my awareness before God like an olive branch. I believe our vulnerability acts as a magnet for God's.

As I make space for Him there, I'll do one of two things: either I'll ask Him to reveal to me what's on His heart in that moment (what He's thinking about or what He'd like to show me), or I'll bring something or someone before Him in my mind's eye to allow it to be seen and acknowledged by Him. As I do this, I stay open not necessarily to pictures, words, answers, or what God may say to make sense of the matter; I listen to His heart, His feelings, His overall sense so I can participate in Him toward that person, place, or situation.

God isn't looking to download information to us like robots; He wants us to jump with joy as He does, to feel the love He has for us and others, and even to grieve for the world like He does. He wants us to be like Him.

I might find myself weeping, laughing, falling in love, or interceding in ways that I can't quite language or make sense of, or I may just feel a lightness that although I sense none of that, or anything at all, God is present and appreciating my willingness.

The greatest fruit in those times is the deep connection I feel with God. It's not always about "being productive" in prayer or even making sense of things. It's about giving God the opportunity to be known by me as He's already allowed Himself to be known.

WATCHING PRAYER

Where listening prayer seeks to participate in feeling God with empathy, compassion, and withness, watching prayer is about allowing God to lead a conversation through pictures, images, stories, or unfolding dramas. Watching prayer is more of a co-labouring creative prayer—like visual storytelling between God and us.

With watching prayer, we similarly open ourselves up to enter into God, but instead of sensing what He's feeling, we're looking for pictures to lead us in how we should pray about a particular issue, person, or place. A bit like a divine dance. It's similar to listening prayer and is a helpful practice when praying for others too.

As a teenager, I spent my weekends in pubs wearing black clothes and dog chains, singing in a melodic rock band. But before all that, believe it or not, I was a Latin American and ballroom dancer—and a national champion of sorts at that. At our intermediate school, we were taught how to samba, rumba, and quickstep, and I, discovering I had a bit of a thing for natural rhythm, decided to take it seriously and compete nationally to become an A-grade champion in Latin American.

In ballroom dancing, both you and your partner learn all the routines down to every second. We used to spend countless hours perfecting routines throughout the year to enter major competitions, and we would work the details right down to our facial gestures. It was almost mathematical.

But despite both partners needing to do all the work and master the whole routine, in ballroom and Latin dancing, it was the men who led. By *led*, I mean, it was on their shoulders to take responsibility for the muscle tension that guided the dancers into particular moves, to hold the frame, and to push into the next stage of each dance.

It wasn't about who was more important or better; it was about the necessity for there to be a leader in every situation. Much like the way we elect a government to lead our countries, they're not better humans than we are nor do they claim to be, but we need someone to lead so others can get on with the work they're called to do. In dancing, the man's role was to lead so the woman would shine. Everyone was meant to watch on in astonishment at the beauty, talent, and wonder of the female dancers.

Watching prayer is like that with a major difference: God leads precisely because He is far greater, more beautiful, more powerful, and wiser than we are. Astonishingly, though, He invites us to co-create with Him in prayer. Because He considers us to be His friends, He invites us to participate in the dance of prayer, moving and shifting to the rhythm of His love and heavenly agenda, and as we do, just like ballroom dancing, we make God shine all the more to the world. We're participating with God, but we're always following.

In watching prayer, I'm opening myself up to see and hear God and what's on His heart first. I am His first responder, waiting for what He'll do. As I wait, I invite the Spirit to speak through pictures, and when He does, I begin to pray around what I see. Often as I pray in this way, the picture morphs or gets added to. Sometimes it becomes more like a movie and I'm following along. What's important isn't so much what I see or how I see it but that, when I do see something, anything, I begin to pray into it gently, using it as a reference.

Say I'm opening myself up to God, and as I wait, I see a picture of a tree. I might say, "Thank You, Father, that You have planted yourself like a tree within me. That You are a tree that is immovable in the world and a tree that others can come to for shade." Then as I continue to pray in that way, I see a rope swing appear. I may respond by saying, "Father, will You help me to rest in Your presence and find joy in just being with You in my life?" I'm beginning to follow God's lead in the dance He's offering me.

But all of a sudden, I may see others walking around the tree with blindfolds on, and I might intercede for the world, "Spirit, I know You long for more to enjoy the joy and freedom that resting in You brings. Would You open the eyes of the blind to see You so they can come and rest? Would You empower me to speak words of invitation, and would You show me who these people are that I can invite them to come to You for shade and relief from the heat and noise of the world?" Now we're full swing in our routine of prayer and communion.

Whether the prayer turns into intercession, thanksgiving, praise, or a conversation about wisdom, the idea of watching prayer is that we're using our mind's eye, our visual faculties, to commune with God and staying in the moment long enough for the Spirit to keep leading, changing, and showing as He desires. As we behold, God is leading and we're following, letting what He's doing be our agenda, but we're also co-creating as we add the layers of our own lives and experiences to our intercession and worship.

Watching prayer may be easier for you if you're more visual or an artist, or if words aren't your main way of expressing yourself or of understanding the world. I've found my ability to connect better with listening or watching prayer can change depending on the season I'm in. But I think what's important is that watching and listening prayer offer us an alternative to a words-exchange-only view of prayer that can inhibit the experience of withness.

THE PRACTICE OF WATCHING PRAYER

If you'd like to practise watching prayer, find a comfortable space where you can be alone and present to God without interruption or distraction. Then begin to open up your heart to God. Imagine Him dwelling within you, and allow your mind to centre on His immanent presence and desire to commune with you.

Ask God to show you His heart and mind and to lead you in prayer. As you begin to have faint pictures, maybe flashes of faint pictures, or what may otherwise feel like imaginations to you, allow elements of those images to inform you in prayer. Don't stress about understanding the details perfectly or worry about getting your biblical dictionary out; respond with the first thoughts and feelings that come to mind. It's often not until we begin praying that things make themselves clearer to us. It's important that we wade into the water, then let the current of Spirit pull us in a little deeper.

As you pray through the images you're seeing, consider what they mean to you personally, who they remind you of, or what they say about God. Allow God to add to them, change them, or inform them as you watch, beholding what you're seeing.

When the natural movement of the images and prayer stops, allow yourself to stop with it. Wait a little while and see if there's anything else that comes up or that God may want to add. This prayer is Spirit led. There's no right amount of time or prayer that's meant to come out of it, and it's not your role to keep it moving. Remember, God is the river, not you.

Once you feel the sense of this particular prayer leave you, be still and enjoy God's peace and rest. Personally, I often find that once the momentum of the prayer leaves me, I can sit with deep restedness and a great sense of God's presence in silence for some time.

PROPHETIC PRAYER

Prophetic prayer is simply any prayer that God begins and leads. It's prayer that follows God's surprising agenda with confidence and attention. Of course, prophetic prayer can be predictive, but it's so much more than that. This kind of prophecy is for everyone, not just prophets or those with the spiritual gift; it's part of the package of being indwelt by the living, breathing God.

At their core, watching and listening prayers are also prophetic prayers because prophecy is making Christ known to a particular people, in a particular place, at a particular time. As our situations change, culture progresses, and we grow, we the church and the world need God and what's on His heart re-presented to us in a way we can grasp and understand.

God is not a theology or an ism, He's a Person, and it takes listening to Him daily to know who He is and what He's doing today. Without prophetic prayer we're left praying yesterday's prayers for today's world and that won't do. Especially in times like these.

Let me share something I felt the Spirit show me in my own watching-prayer time. One morning as I was opening myself up to God to ask Him what was on His heart, I saw a picture of a river. I saw that as I entered the river, the current got stronger the deeper I went. I felt God saying that I wasn't the river, so it wasn't my job to create the current for the energy to make the journey downstream. The river was God, and it's His constant flow, His power, His reality that I'm invited to lean into and navigate when I pray.

Then He showed me two ways I could engage with Him there that I shared with you earlier in the book: either float or canoe. Floating is the adoration and abiding that Christ invites me into. It's lying on the water's surface with trust that God's goodness and love are strong enough to take me downstream as I look up at the sky and admire the surroundings. This is the beholding life; it's worship and admiration without any further agenda.

But the other way we navigate the waters is to carry our canoe, paddle, and partner with God in the journey downstream. Here, we're using the skills and gifts God has given us to navigate the eddies, rapids, and obstacles of the journey. This could be our watching, listening, and prophetic prayer.

Prophetic prayer, then, is our following the lead of the river, much like the ballroom-dancing metaphor, to bring God's plans of fulfilment into being in creation. Not only as spectators or floating vessels, but as craftsmen who can navigate the waters of God as we go. We're working, yes, but we're working in response to God's current, and that will give us divine energy.

Ultimately, all of history is floating downstream toward God's perfect ending of renewal. Our role is to navigate with God by responding to the rocks, the weather, the currents, and the channels that the world throws at us whilst staying squarely in the Spirit's waters. By watching and listening to God, we're responding to the unique map of our time and flowing with God in the ways that He longs to, right now, in our world.

Prayer, then, in many ways is the spiritual practice of response. What makes it prophetic is when it's a personal response to God and not led only by our theology or assumptions. In other words, prayer is what flows from beholding the world through God being poised and ready to thank, intercede, worship, grieve, ask, knock, or share Him in the many events of our days.

Prayer is primarily a response because we are born into a moving world, made by a God who has been moving Himself far longer than we have. Prayer, then, is our joining in the motion of both God and the world and our participation by blessing that world as we're pulled along by it and God.

Prophetic prayer is about stopping, waiting, and beholding God and others regularly enough to respond to Him or them and their needs, joy, grief, longing, or sickness. We wake to a new day and respond with prayerful gratitude. We encounter a sick person and respond by praying for their healing there and then. We're confronted with hate or crisis and respond by interceding for those affected and inviting God to move powerfully.

All of these are co-labouring responses to the world already moving around us. They're prophetic prayers because they're applying the alive Christ, the Christ who is alive and well in us, to historical needs and because "the testimony of Jesus is the spirit of prophecy."[48]

There's a powerful lightness and freedom that comes with prophetically praying. It's alive and exciting, but it's restful too. It's not a striving disposition; it births healthy intercessors. It's in this kind of prayer that beholding naturally bridges the two worlds of charismatic and contemplative, offering a wonder to participate in and a responsibility in the world.

Through watching and listening prayer, we're learning to become a prophetic people. Who not only hear what God has to say but feel how He feels too. We're learning to participate with God in what He's doing in the world, paddling down the river of His creative love, doing our part to bring Him into the world.

But as importantly as any of that, we're deepening our communion together by being with Him in the process.

Chapter 11

PRAYING WITH OUR BODIES

"Father, hear my body pray."

Prayer Vol. 03

"As the deer pants for streams of water,
so my soul pants for you, my God.
My soul thirsts for God, for the living God."[49]

At the dawn of human history, as the angelic host stood poised to witness the Divine Hongi between God and man, we're not told that human spirits stood waiting there too, excited to be inserted into the soil-shaped bodies God had fashioned. We're told that when God breathed into the shape of man, humanity awakened, created, unified spiritually, emotionally, and physically simultaneously: "Then the LORD God formed a man from the dust of the ground and breathed into his nostrils the breath of life, and the man became a living being."[50]

The spirit and the body were created together, and it was this unified whole that God called "human." It was to us, in our bodies, that God gave the Divine Hongi, and our bodies, as much as our minds, participate in the wonder of a beholding life.

A number of years ago I learned this in a powerful way.

Over time, one of the struggles I've had to navigate with my health is the constant brain fog chronic suffering causes. Brain fog, as the name suggests, is a mental malaise where it's hard to string sentences together, remember important dates, times, and facts, and to make sense of the world around you. It's kind of a right hook when you're sick, because at a time when ongoing illness is beckoning extra mental strength to stay positive, your mind is at its weakest to do so. That's why I started writing so much. Journaling and writing prayers helped to distil all that and show me my own thoughts, my own prayers, when they were otherwise cyclonic in my mind.

The problem for me was, I would go through seasons where brain fog and constant illness didn't just last several weeks, or even a month or two, but sometimes three, four, or five months at a time. I wanted to know and walk with God, but my ability to come to Him through my mind would painfully obscure the journey.

It was particularly bad one year when I had to eat gluten to be tested for coeliac disease. I'd been off gluten for seven years because it clearly made me ill, but a recent diagnosis of osteoporosis meant the doctors needed to officially test it to be sure. I had to eat gluten every day for six weeks, and in all honesty, I turned into the living dead. Not only for six weeks, but for the months of recovery afterward all I could do was sit in a chair in the living room day and night, hardly able to talk to anyone, struggling for the energy to even stand up.

My body was utterly spent and struggling to recover from the poisoning gluten had brought to my system. That damage meant too that my mind was in a difficult place; as recent discoveries in neuroscience have shown, if you attack the gut, you attack the mind. Anxiety, depression, and mental fatigue became severe.

I'd expected it to happen because I'd been there before, so I'd prepared myself mentally. I kept telling myself at the start of it all that I didn't need to listen to the feelings of downness and anxiety. I told my mind that my body just needed grace, to give it time. But as one month turned into two, three, and eventually four, it became harder to do. I struggled to pray, I couldn't sense or see God at all, and my mind was too foggy to theologise my way through it. I was in trouble, longing for God, needing respite, aching to hear His voice.

I distinctly remember one day, in the pain of it all, lying in bed midafternoon, frustrated that I couldn't sense or reach God, and in an act of final relent, I simply exhaled, "Father, hear my body pray." It sort of came from nowhere when I said it—maybe it was really the Spirit teaching me how to pray—but as the words left my mind, a deep relief passed over me. Even though I was unable to consciously commune with God due to mental exhaustion and fatigue, my body was crying out, interceding for me on my behalf. And it was.

I realised that God was more than able to see the pain and struggle of my body laid out before Him, crying out for healing and redemption. In that prayer, I was asking God to hear my body as petition and, as importantly, intercession for the world full of others who were sick and struggling. When my mind wasn't strong enough to say what it needed, my body was able.

I had another experience around that time which helped shape my understanding of body prayer even more deeply, this time with my eldest son. On this day I'd taken him to the rugby fields so he could play with some of his teammates. They're all older than he is, and all much closer as friends. We'd just moved to this small beachside town a year earlier, and my son was still earning his stripes with the boys.

On this day, that was as obvious as ever. They excluded him, relegating him to the sidelines of their game whilst they all played on. I was sitting in my car for an hour, watching with a mixture of anger and heartbreak, and I could see he was feeling the same. He stood there for that whole hour excluded until they all decided to go home without giving him a turn. When he got back to the car, I asked him how it went, expecting him to open up to me about what he was feeling, but instead he just quietly said, "Yeah, good, Dad."

He was only eight years old, and I'm not sure that he even really understood everything he was feeling. He was stoked to spend time with his friends, he looked up to them, but he probably also felt a whole bunch of things inside that he couldn't articulate: embarrassment, disappointment, loneliness, anger, or even a little shame.

He was wearing all of it, and it was obvious to me. But I'm older; I know how to make sense of and articulate that stuff, and he's still learning. His posture, his tone of voice, his silence even, told me what he either didn't know or was unable to tell me out loud. His body spoke to me.

All the drive home I found ways to tell him how proud I was of his character, to laugh together, and to subtly remind him that with me he's never alone and never excluded. That he's deeply loved. He didn't need to explain it all to me; his body said it all.

You could say that, in a way, my son's body was praying to me—aching for love, calling out for encouragement and healing—and as his father, I was able to see and respond to it even when it wasn't verbalised. I could pick up from his body what he was unable to explain mentally and emotionally, and because I'm his dad, that was more than enough for me to love him through the moment.

If I, as a broken earthly dad, can hear my son's life and body as prayer, how much more can our perfect heavenly Father? That's what I mean by allowing my body to pray. It's trusting that my own body beholds and is beheld by God too, not because I'm always able to consciously articulate it, but because God is a good Father who in His infinite wisdom and maturity is loving and caring enough to answer the prayers and inner movements I don't even know how to express.

I wonder if this is what the psalmist meant when he prayed, "As the deer pants for streams of water, so my soul pants for you, my God. My soul thirsts for God, for the living God."[51] The thirst for water is an all-body experience. It's a dehydrated ache, a dry-mouthed, life-threatening longing for the very thing that brings life to our bodies. A deer pants for water with its whole being.

The word the psalmist used for "soul" here is *nephesh*, a Hebrew word that literally translates as "throat." It's a word often used in the Old Testament for what we translate as "soul," and it refers to the whole person, mind, body, emotions, and even relationships, as one unified thing. *Nephesh* means our entire existence, not just some disembodied spirit floating around inside somewhere.

So when the psalmist writes that his soul, his *nephesh*, longs for God the way a deer does water, I imagine he's referring to this kind of all-body prayer. The kind of body prayer that I was experiencing lying on my bed that day, desperate for the waters of the Spirit to meet not only my inner life, but my very physical need for His healing too. My barren body was crying out for God in its own language. Its very lack inviting God's gracious care. Our bodies long for the living God as much as our minds do.

RECONNECTING WITH OUR BODIES

Part of the great disconnection of our times has been a disconnection from our own bodies. On one hand, we have magazines, podcasts, and blogs full of how to eat right, slim down, meditate for positive mental outcomes, or otherwise become comfortable with the bodies we have. On the other hand, in much of Western mainline church at least, we seem to have relegated our bodies to our non-God lives and left them out of prayer. We've bought into Enlightenment thinking that the body is just the machine that hosts the real stuff—the conscious self—and isn't a meaningful participant in our communion with God.

But beholding God involves our bodies in powerful ways, and to stand or sit before Him, we need to restore our relationship to them.

This parsing out of our person into two separate entities, one being more important than the other, is what philosophers call the "Cartesian split," or "the two-story person," and could be loosely summarized as the belief that the mind or unseen substances of a person are at odds with the physical, seen, and felt.

In this view, the essence of a person is essentially the invisible stuff, the physical parts are just the organic machine it inhabits. As the idea developed in Western psychology and philosophy, it came to mean that the mind is what makes us human, what makes us special. The thesis of this belief being demonstrated in the famous statement by French philosopher René Descartes, "I think, therefore I am."

Inheritors of this view, of which many of us are, would be tempted to believe that the body, then, has nothing to say in prayer or in our spiritual lives other than to be a hurdle to overcome. The mind is where we commune with God; the body and its natural needs are a nuisance.

As Christians, however, we believe the opposite. Not only because of the incarnation and what we've already explored through a Eucharistic vision of the world, but because the Bible is full of body use in spiritual worship. Theology is essentially theory until it meets the real-life decisions of our active lives, and the New Testament calls our *bodies* "temples of the Holy Spirit," not our *brains*.[52]

Circumcision is a concrete example of that, the ultimate identifier of a Hebrew man to God. The new covenant only requires circumcision of the heart, but James also made clear in his oft-quoted assertion "for as the body without the spirit is dead, so faith without works is dead also"[53] that heart faith is demonstrated by the body through works in order to be authentic.

Throughout the Old Testament the Hebrew words we translate as "worship" and "praise" in English are often rooted in acts that involve the body. *Shachah*, commonly translated as "worship," means "to prostrate oneself," as in lying down flat before God and reverencing Him. *Yadah*, often translated as "praise," means "to hold out the hand," again especially in reverence. The word *barak*, which is translated as "blessing" in the Psalms (as in, our blessing God), means "to kneel before," and the word *abad*, which is translated again as "worship" in Exodus 3:12, implies "to work for" or "to serve."

The Old Testament uses many other words for "worship" and "praise," not all of them involving the body, but the focus on the body and bodily acts as a way of loving and worshipping God is vital to a psalmic understanding of prayer. Not to mention the direct calls to raise our hands, shout, or sing found throughout.

In the New Testament we see Jesus reinforcing the importance of fasting, which is another form of body prayer. Those who encountered Him worshipped Jesus by dropping down in front of Him, and before His burial, Jesus' body was prepared by Mary with an expensive jar of perfume.

Ultimately, it was Christ's physical act of being spread out on the cross that demonstrated the lengths He would go for us in love, and the resurrection of that same physical body that is our ultimate hope. His act of communion and worship to God was the greatest physical sacrifice any person could ever make. With all this in mind, it's strange that we are less inclined to make the sign of the cross or to see our bodies, without conscious mental dialogue, as participating in prayer.

Beholding is about changing that and giving God our bodies.

Our bodies long for the living God
as much as our minds do.

Sadly, due to Enlightenment-influenced thought on the split between soul and body, slowly but surely much of the physical and often liturgical forms of prayer that the church has practised for thousands of years have been labeled as "religious" in a derogatory sense. As in, actions that are meaningless to a heart faith, actions that are trying to earn what only the heart can offer. Admittedly, we can see a beautiful truth there in that doing things without love is hollow and empty, but the heart follows the hand as much as the hand the heart.[54]

Sometimes, doing things gives shape to our love in a way that emotions and thinking alone can't. For us in a beholding life, this means what we do with our bodies is as much a form of prayer as our minds and hearts. Kneeling when you don't feel anything in your heart still means something to God, as does reading prayers, raising your hands to God in song, and taking Eucharist when it doesn't make mental sense or carry the kind of engaged mystical wonder we may want it to.

We can allow our bodies to free us from the bondage of our emotions, and even sometimes our minds, by loving in the way we live, in the way we bring ourselves to our neighbors, Sunday church, and ultimately to prayer. When we do, we're practising beholding God with it all.

This is also why it matters so much to God what we do with our bodies in our day to day. Our bodies are the homes of God. How we position them says something about our beholding manner before Him in our ordinary activities, and when we refuse to use them for selfish gain, for lust, or for injustice, this too is spiritual prayer and worship. It makes obedience to Christ's commands less about obedience to a law and more about conforming to the image of Love already within us. It's us treating our bodies as they truly, theologically are.

Few places in Scripture have illustrated this personally to me as poignantly as Isaiah 58. The passage starts with God telling the prophet to cry out and declare to Israel their sin before going on about how they pray and fast all day and night wanting to seek God's face. Already, if the readers are paying attention, they'll notice how bizarre that is. How could God say that a people who seek His face day and night through prayer and fasting are sinful?

Many of us today would consider them the "spiritual ones," the ones with a heart after God's own, the alive ones. But not God. Because as the prophet went on, God accused them of seeking Him in prayer like that only to go and propagate injustices when they left their prayer closets. They verbally hurt one another, contributed to an unjust economy, and failed to pay people fairly or care for the sick and lonely. "You cannot fast as you do today," God said, "and expect your voice to be heard on high."[55]

God was accusing His people of being "spiritual" in a detached, non-Eucharistic way. They were beholding God in conscious prayer but not with their bodies, and that wasn't enough. Their bodies needed to pray too. If they did that, said the prophet, "if you do away with the yoke of oppression, with the pointing finger and malicious talk, and if you spend yourselves in behalf of the hungry and satisfy the needs of the oppressed, then your light will rise in the darkness." Then, he said, "you will call, and the LORD will answer."[56]

Is this tit-for-tat transactional spirituality? Not at all. God wasn't saying they needed to obey to receive His love; that would be a cynical reading, and it would be misunderstanding God's longing for reconciliation. This was God saying that mental prayer and the inner desire to behold Him must be lived through a life that beholds Him in the other by seeking to reconcile, heal, and bring justice wherever it is left broken. It is impossible to behold God and live unaffected in an unjust world. Prayer is both.

When we participate in Christ's work of reconciliation with the world, whether that's through the distribution of wealth, befriending lonely neighbors, keeping our bodies from lustful behavior, offering hospitality to newcomers in town, healing racial hurt, loving our children selflessly, or forgiving our spouses, we're beholding God in others, in the systems of our world and in our own bodies. We're worshipping with our whole lives; we're praying with our bodies. Or as St Paul would say, "offer[ing] [our] bodies as a living sacrifice, holy and pleasing to God … [our] true and proper worship."[57]

When we hold up and live our lives before God like this, everything becomes prayer. Everything becomes communion.

PRACTISING BODY PRAYER

The praying body can be liberating to those of us who struggle to keep thoughts together. Plenty of people find it problematic to sit and think their way to God, not only due to a short attention span, but because of ongoing battles with depression, anxiety, or a crisis of faith. Communion comes under threat every time we depend only on our minds to commune with God.

There are many seasons in our walking in the way of Jesus when our bodies' trauma, illness, or aches carry the potential to hinder our communion with God. It's during these times that our physical acts of prostration, kneeling, and sitting before God in silence can really carry us. Especially when we bring our heart to it. Body prayer is an invitation to an embodied communion through any and all seasons we face.

That's important to me, because all the theology of beholding God with my body I've shared here came after my experience of it. For me, learning body prayer was a necessity. "Father, hear my body pray" was my way of saying, "Lord, my mind is out to sea, and I can't trust it. I can't think straight, I can't see, and I desperately long to live in communion with You. So, today, hear the aches and pains of my body as intercession and petition. See my rest as an invitation to be with me. I'm too exhausted, too foggy to say it aloud, let my body be enough. Allow what my body is doing to say more than my mind can. Hear my body pray."

What we do with our bodies is as much a form of prayer as our minds and hearts. Kneeling when you don't feel anything in your heart still means something to God.

In that moment communion became about an unspoken knowing between us. God rushed in like a loving parent to hear my body crying for healing, redemption, and union with Him. He met me in sickness and carried what I couldn't carry. As I prayed that prayer over and over, I sensed His closeness and the connection we have with others when I sat with them in their pain too. Communion went deeper; it transcended conscious mental dialogue and it bled a little more, again, into the whole of my life.

But it also opened me up to other practices. I find myself more and more making the sign of the cross as a physical act of prayer. The sign of the cross, I discovered, is a common form of prayer for the church dating back to the second century. The practice involves pinching the thumb and forefingers together, with your pinky and finger beside it tucked to your palm. The thumb and two fingers together represent the Father, Son, and Holy Spirit, and the two tucked fingers the divine and human nature of Jesus. Then, bringing the hand first to the forehead, then the sternum, then your left and right shoulders, you make the sign of the cross over your chest.

St Francis of Assisi would do this without even saying words as a way of praying for the sick, healing many. It can be done as often as you remember as a way of bringing your body into God-awareness or as a physical way of embracing Christ. It can be done as you enter a prayer space or as you begin or end a prayer. If you, like me, are from a nontraditional background, it may feel strange at first, but it grows with use and becomes a practice of real meaning. It changes how I feel about my body when I pray this way. It awakens my awareness to its holiness. To the God it homes.

Other forms of body prayer to practise include kneeling as an act of submission and relent to what God is asking of us. It could mean lying flat, facedown on the floor in adoration or humility before God. Sometimes when I feel something I can't name, and I don't know what to pray, I lie on my front like that for extended periods of time. I let my body say there what I can't form in words, what I can't make sense of.

At times, I'll stand as a gesture of confidence and courage. Often, I stand if I'm really interceding for someone or boldly asking God for an answer to prayer or for provision, or to receive His Spirit in some special way. Standing whilst I pray like that shows my at-readiness and confidence in God to hear me when I pray for others. Engaging our bodies in our prayer is a beautiful way of connecting us with ourselves and gives depth and meaning to our communion with God. A way of beholding Him with all of us, because although our minds are important, we're so much more than them too.

We may feel something when we do all these things, and that's great. But even if we don't, God hears our bodies praying in this way. It means something. It gives our bodies a role in beholding the ever-living majesty of God. It shows Him that with every inch of us, we love Him.

A GOSPEL FOR THE MIND-MARGINAL

This brings me to one final thought on how powerful praying with our bodies can be to our understanding and moving through the world. Because if living life with chronic sickness and the limitations it brings has taught me anything, it's how easy it is for people who don't fit the standard mold to be accidentally unnoticed by a strong, fast-paced world around them. It's often not until one feels or becomes marginalised, or until they suffer, that they discover truths that weren't evident in their strength.

Coming to terms with body prayer and my own mental limitations brought one such revelation to my own life; that is, what the gospel has to say to those more severely mentally disadvantaged than I, and in return, what they can teach us about the deep power of divine communion.

As we've already seen, one of the unfortunate side effects of living in a post-Enlightenment world is the way we attribute value to the mind over the body. This can have a very tangible negative effect on those in society for whom the mind is a difficult or debilitating place. This is true along the entire spectrum from those suffering mental breakdowns, depression, and anxiety through to the autistic or those who have suffered severe brain injuries.

What does Jesus have to say to someone who, as we see it, has lost the full capacity of their brain? If a human being can't have conscious mental dialogue with God, or at least if their mind is their place of greatest pain, are they still able to pray and to know Him? Or are they relegated to a second-level heavenly citizen status? How do our gatherings both on Sunday and in other parts of our community life offer prayerful and worshipful space for those who feel disconnected or troubled by our usual practices? And how do we help them see how valued and adored their acts of body prayer are to God?

I believe understanding the importance of body prayer offers a redeeming and humanising theology for these deeply loved of God. Not only because they need to hear it, but because we do too. *We* need to see and be taught the wonder and magnificence of God through those who see His face in ways many of us can't. *We* need to consider these in our communities when we're gathering on Sundays for communal worship, or when we're considering issues of justice in society and *we* ourselves need the depth and beauty that a gospel like this can offer us. Because we need to share the gospel and live the gospel with them.

Jesus didn't come to save and reconcile minds; He came to save and reconcile people. That includes those whose minds are a war field or who are profoundly different from the majority. To limit prayer, or worship, or discipleship with Christ to mental growth alone, or to underdevelop a theology of the body—of body worship and body prayer—is to do an injustice to those unseen because of their experiencing the world differently. Looking only toward brilliant thinkers for God and away from the *other* is to miss the living God who is so profoundly discovered among them.

I've learned both through my consideration of the wonder of those who don't have the advantage of that kind of communication, and through my own, at times, disabling sickness, that beholding God is so much more than what our minds can do. It's about positioning our bodies before God, allowing them to be seen by Him in our highs and lows, and letting them invite His love, grace, and healing when our minds are no longer the safe places they once were.

Chapter 12

BECOMING BEHOLDERS

"Open my eyes to see, Holy Spirit,
the Life behind all life,
the Breath behind all breath,
the Unseen behind the seen,
that I would behold the world as You do,
and not as I've been taught."

Prayer Vol. 03

This book has told the story of how my life was transformed through crisis. A crisis that helped me move from a transactional relationship with God to a friendship. It's a story of submission, really, of a relent to the beauty of God and how that set off a chain reaction that led to an entirely different way of being and seeing than I'd ever experienced.

A deepening of my experience in God.

A beholding life.

But there is another story too. A story of newness stumbling its way into our communities. A story of an invitation to a different way of being with God alone and in the church. I got my first tastes of that story during my years as prayer curator at Central Vineyard Church in the latter years of the season this book is centred on. It was there that I first started weekly early-morning communion services. I didn't know a thing about Eucharist, or Real Presence. I'd had no exposure to liturgy in my life at all, but deep down, because of my story, I knew that it held a key to what God was doing.

Those first communion mornings were awkward. I copied and pasted a liturgy together from patchy Google searches, made everyone stand around a small table in the dark at 7.00 a.m. on cold winter mornings, and read my way through it. None of that mattered, though, the Spirit seemed to make it alive. Eventually, someone with an Anglican background helped me navigate my way through it with a little more class.

After running prayer meetings for a good year or two with no success, suddenly a little community of a dozen people were showing up week to week to sit in front of some lit candles in silence, read liturgy, and take communion together. Eventually, it even became a place for the surrounding community to come to. People who didn't go to church came along and had profound experiences of God.

It radically transformed me. The real grace in that meal had a tangible effect on my joy, sense of God, and love for others.

Later, a friend from the same church came back from a weekend retreat centred on the Prodigal Son journey and suggested we do something similar in our own community. Again, we didn't really know what we were doing, but we gave it a shot. We booked a venue out in the dense native forest of the Kaimai Range, and twenty people showed up to spend time in silence, community, and prayerful reflection. It was powerful. In fact, it was the most powerful form of ministry I'd ever experienced.

Instead of a conference stage with an eloquent speaker, there was silence that made room for the gentle voice of God to speak to us personally. Instead of breakaway seminars in side rooms, there were deep and meaningful conversations over tea during long breaks where the stories of our lives helped one another be seen. Instead of an altar call, there was a sending call: go and be with your Father, let Him embrace you. Instead of consumer Christianity, the retreat offered us space to do the hard work of coming to God ourselves.

Eventually, I started to run more retreats through my own ministry, Commoners Communion, and I experienced people of all ages from all church backgrounds having profound and yet totally ordinary experiences with God together. It never ceases to amaze me how these very earthy and unflashy weekends often come to shift the trajectory of our lives toward deeper divine knowing.

On another one-day silent retreat our church ran, one person told me they felt the arms of God around them for the first time in their lives. Another, a young mum with three children, fell asleep for hours during the deep silence period and called it the truest rest she'd had in years. One person finally forgave someone they'd been unable to forgive for almost a decade. All without any teaching, hype, or interpersonal prayer ministry.

The more we entrusted people to God, it seemed, the more room we gave Him to do what He does best.

We were stumbling our way through a transition from our evangelical, charismatic, and nondenominational backgrounds into something profound. It was a work of the Spirit. Not that we were leaving behind all the other stuff that made us who we were. We still did worship nights, led prophetic groups, did street mission, and Sunday church as usual, but we brought in more space for abiding with God amidst it all. We welcomed what tradition had to teach us. And this in a church of some three hundred young adults. The very people I'm often told aren't interested in all that "religious" stuff.

I'd spent the first half of my role in that community trying to rally people to prayer meetings to seek God's presence and intercede for the world, not realising how tired, uncertain, and God-weary they were. I was asking them to run before they could walk. Then, when I couldn't get someone along to a free thirty-minute prayer meeting before church on Sunday mornings, dozens of young adults were paying seventy dollars each to attend a one-day silent retreat at a monastery to learn how to rest in and be with God. And the reservations were selling out fast.

It was then that I started to see that for too long we had failed to pass on the basic practices of life *in* God.

Ultimately, that's what becoming a beholding people is. It's about remembering and practising what it means to abide in God, then passing it on to future generations. So many of our churches have rallied people to go, to serve in church, to think, do, and be more without teaching them how to sit with God first. With our best intentions, over time, we came to place the Great Commandment over and above the Great Commission and we burned people out.

These stories aren't the only stories either, they're just the ones *I* can tell. The recent hunger for spiritual practices (or disciplines) in our generation is an encouraging sign that we want change. We see that without that change we'll keep missing out on becoming like the God we love and long for so much. I know many other communities are embracing being with God as central to who they are and are doing the hard work of teaching the next generation of God lovers to behold.

The invitation of our time, I believe, is to go back to the start again, to our first love, and to teach the church how to pray. Not prayer as we've known it. Not the transactional-only stuff. But the bread of our faith, our sitting with and beholding God. It's a call for us as individuals to take up God's invitation to a Eucharistic life, to the Divine Hongi, and for our church communities to create shared spaces that foster this reality.

As I sit here at my desk writing, over seven years on now from when my journey with chronic illness became a big part of my story, I'm unable to sing again. It's been that way for over a year. Around me, I can hear the waves meeting the shoreline outside my cabin, and rain is touching down gently on the roof above me. Life feels profoundly still.

I'm not sure anymore what my future holds. My body tells a different story to my heart. My body may one day, in this life, regain all its strength and I might be able to look back on this long journey as a story to be told in past tense. I may not.

I may sing again. I may not.

What I do know is this: I've been gifted with a life that in whatever state it may continue is full of God's love. I am never alone. I've found what I was made for, to gaze into the God of beauty and to find Him gazing back at me with His eyes of knowing love. To receive this life as sacred.

This is my song, and I believe it's yours too. To behold, and to be held by our heavenly Father, forever.

ACKNOWLEDGEMENTS

Through all of the years of wrestle, beauty, and change this book emerges from, there have been people whose friendship and love were like oxygen to me. Katie, your love and strength are the stuff of legends. This book is as much yours as it is mine. To my sons, Mikal, Theodore, and Finley, you have lived this story too, painting my life with joy. I hope this book can become a friend to you in the years to come, guiding you to the Father who has captivated my life.

Dean McQuoid, our weekly breakfasts were often all the social engagement I had during those tough years. Your words strengthened me, and your flame for God inspires me still. To Mark Donovan, who was the first to get the original version of this book and encouraged me to keep going, it's hard to understate how your friendship has helped me to keep sharing what God has put on my heart with the world.

Whilst this book was still a small collection of essays titled "An Invitation to Spiritual Renewal in Our Time," I passed it along to my friend John Mark Comer to see if he'd be interested in writing a little foreword. Instead, he passed it on to some industry friends and made connections resulting in this book being in your hands today. I'd never dreamed of publishing this as a book; it's here today because of your encouragement and belief. Thank you, for that and the years of friendship we've had together.

Andrew Killick, my friend and editor of my three prayer volumes, read over the initial script of this book, sitting with it and helping me sense-make it during its earliest (and messiest!) conception. Thank you, brother, for that and for helping me to become a better writer and thinker over these years.

There are so many others who have held me up through the years this story straddles. To the incredible Magee family, how could we ever repay you for the hope, sustenance, and generosity you gave our family? You showed up out of nowhere and showed us Christ. Thank you. Richard Gandy, who helped open the States to me as a musician and ended up becoming a lifelong friend. Jon Class, for helping me bring the heart of this message to song and words. The Sheeds, Wisemans, and the rest of the Central Vineyard whānau, who as a church wrapped themselves around us when we had nothing. You brought us food, fixed our house, paid our power bills, and were Christ to us in the most real way. Our journeys are intertwined.

To Vaughan Park and the staff there, who showed me hospitality and the stillness of God when I couldn't do anything else, thank you for being a home for my spiritual transformation. To Bishop Bruce Gilberd, who has become a close friend and mentor these past few years, thank you for your time, wisdom, and encouragement in my prayer journey.

I'd like to thank my friends Aaron Hardy and Bradford Haami for reading over my chapter on the Divine Hongi and for guiding my posture toward the beauty that is te ao Māori. Also, Nick Bannister (resident theologian at David C Cook) and Bishop Bruce Gilberd, for your help with "The Importance of Eating God," helping me to deliver a complex and confronting chapter with as much grace as possible.

This book is the fruit of a team of people for whom I'm truly grateful—Estee, Andrea, and The Bindery team, thank you for believing in this work enough to find it a home. Too, Michael and Stephanie, you haven't just edited and shaped this book with me, you've believed in it as much as I have. That's meant more than you know, thank you. To the rest of the crew at David C Cook—Katie, James, and Jack, thank you for your amazing work. Without all of you, all this would have remained a few strange essays floating through the intersphere.

There are so many others who belong to this story. People who supported us financially through tough years, who have prayed for us, encouraged us, and cheerled us the whole way through. We are who we are because of you, this story is yours as well. Thank you all, truly.

NOTES

1. Jeremiah 6:16.

2. James 1:4.

3. This quote is unanimously attributed to Antoine de Saint-Exupéry, likely a paraphrase or alternate translation from his book *Citadelle* (Paris: Gallimard, 1948), sect. LXXV, 687.

4. John 15:15 ERV.

5. Psalm 27:4 ESV.

6. Zephaniah 3:17.

7. John 15:9.

8. Matthew 22:37–40.

9. John 15:9 CEB; Matthew 28:20; Romans 5:5; Zephaniah 3:17.

10. 1 John 4:7–8.

11. Galatians 5:22–23.

12. John 7:37–38.

13. John 14:20.

14. 1 Thessalonians 5:17 ESV.

15. Francis and Kaiora Tipene, *Tikanga: Living with the Traditions of te ao Māori* (Rosedale, New Zealand: HarperCollins, 2021).

16. Cleve Barlow, *Tikanga Whakaaro: Key Concepts in Māori Culture* (Oxford, UK: Oxford University Press, 1991).

17. Hiwi and Pat Tauroa, *Te Marae: A Guide to Customs and Protocol* (New York: Penguin, 2009).

18. 1 Thessalonians 5:17 ESV.

19. Luke 18:38; Luke 18:13 ESV.

20. Quoted in Frederica Mathewes-Green, *The Illumined Heart: Capture the Vibrant Faith of Ancient Christians* (Brewster, MA: Paraclete Press, 2007), 70.

21. Mathewes-Green, *Illumined Heart*, 73.

22. Anthony M. Coniaris, *A Beginner's Introduction to the Philokalia* (Minneapolis, MN: Light & Life, 2017), 63.

23. Psalm 139.

24. Matthew 22:37–40.

25. 1 John 1.

26. John 6:53.

27. John 6:53–54.

28. 1 Corinthians 10:16.

29. St Justin Martyr, chapter 66 in *First Apology*.

30. Irenaeus, *Against Heresies*, 4:33–32.

31. St Augustine, *Sermons*, 227.

32. 2 Corinthians 5:17.

33. John 1:18 NLT.

34. Luke 14:15.

35. 1 Corinthians 11:25 NLT.

36. Mark 4:19.

37. Quoted in Coniaris, *Beginners Introduction to the Philokalia*, 31.

38. Habakkuk 2:20.

39. John 1:18.

40. Psalm 18:11 KJV.

41. Eulalia Peris, "Noise Pollution Is a Major Problem, Both for Human Health and the Environment," European Environment Agency, March 2020, www.eea.europa.eu/articles/noise-pollution -is-a-major#:~:text=Looking%20at%20the%20current%20data ,suffer%20chronic%20high%20sleep%20disturbance.

42. Psalm 105:4 MSG.

43. John 14:23.

44. John 3:3.

45. Psalm 139:1–4.

46. Henri Nouwen, *Out of Solitude: Three Meditations on the Christian Life* (Notre Dame, IN: Ava Maria Press, 2004), 38.

47. Curt Thompson, *Anatomy of the Soul: Surprising Connections between Neuroscience and Spiritual Practices That Can Transform Your Life and Relationships* (Carol Stream, IL: SaltRiver, 2010), xiv.

48. Revelation 19:10 ESV.

49. Psalm 42:1–2.

50. Genesis 2:7.

51. Psalm 42:1–2.

52. 1 Corinthians 6:19.

53. James 2:26 KJV.

54. So articulately demonstrated by James K. A. Smith in his book *You Are What You Love*.

55. Isaiah 58:4.

56. Isaiah 58:9–10.

57. Romans 12:1.

ABOUT THE AUTHOR

Strahan Coleman is a writer, spiritual director, and award-winning musician from Aotearoa, New Zealand. After spending ten years recording and travelling as a folk artist, he founded Commoners Communion in 2017, a ministry exploring conversations in Christian spirituality. Since then he has given himself to his passion of helping others deepen their experience in God through his writing, podcast, spiritual retreats, and online prayer schools. He has published three prayer books, *Prayer Vol. 01, 02,* and *03*, poetic devotionals inviting the reader into a deeper honesty, vulnerability, and closeness with God.

Strahan currently lives by the beach in the Coromandel in Aotearoa, New Zealand with his wife, Katie, and three sons, Mikal, Theodore, and Finley.

Follow Strahan's Ministry:

www.commonerscommunion.com
Instagram: @commoners_communion, @strahanmusic
Spotify: Strahan

BIBLE CREDITS